A CBT Approach to Mental Health Problems in Psychosis

DR EMMA WILLIAMS

BSc (Liverpool), MPhil (Edinburgh), PhD (Liverpool)
Consultant Clinical Psychologist

Routledge
Taylor & Francis Group
LONDON AND NEW YORK

First published 2013 by Speechmark Publishing Ltd.

Published 2017 by Routledge
2 Park Square, Milton Park, Abingdon, Oxon OX14 4RN
711 Third Avenue, New York, NY 10017, USA

Routledge is an imprint of the Taylor & Francis Group, an informa business

Typeset by Darkriver Design, Auckland, New Zealand
British Library Cataloguing in Publication Data
A catalogue record for this book is available from the British Library

ISBN 9780863889677 (pbk)

Contents

About the author

Dr Emma Williams is a Consultant Clinical Psychologist. She has worked with people with psychosis for over 20 years. Her interests are in the promotion of understanding, and development of treatments with an ethical foundation, in order to improve the acceptability and efficacy of NHS provision for people with psychosis. She has lectured both nationally and internationally and taught on Clinical Psychology training courses in England and Scotland. She has published widely including two previous books with Speechmark, *Anger Control Training* with Rebecca Barlow (1998) and *Interventions for Schizophrenia* (2004). She lives and works in Oxfordshire.

Acknowledgements

This book draws together the various treatments available for negative symptoms, emotional and mood disorders in psychosis. It would not have been possible without the pioneering work of many clinicians who have described and developed treatments for this client group from their own specialist fields, knowledge and experience. In particular I am indebted to the work of David Kingdon, Douglas Turkington, Aaron Beck, Neil Rector and colleagues (negative symptoms), Brock Chisholm, Nadine Keen, Craig Steel and Anthony Morrison and his colleagues (PTSD), Adrian Wells (OCD), Steven Jones (mood disturbance) and Max Birchwood (emotional disorders). I am grateful to the many people with a diagnosis of psychosis with whom I have had the pleasure to work; their insights, courage and openness have been humbling.

For Loris: My love goes with you
as your love stays with me.

Introduction

This book goes beyond the traditional treatment focus of cognitive behavioural therapy (CBT) for psychosis, that of positive psychotic symptoms, to address a range of co-occurring mental health problems experienced by people with psychosis. As such it is the only handbook which focuses solely on the assessment and treatment of emotional and mood disorders in people with a diagnosis of psychosis. In addition the central role of stress in the exacerbation of symptoms and the important, but often overlooked, problems associated with negative symptoms are addressed.

The idea for this handbook emerged from many years of working with people with a diagnosis of psychosis who described long-standing problems with social anxiety, depression, obsessive-compulsive symptoms, post-traumatic stress disorder (PTSD) and mood disturbance. These concerns frequently remained untreated despite regular, and often long-term, contact with mental health services. Faced with the overt symptoms of hearing voices or delusional beliefs, many mental health professionals, myself included, tended to focus upon these psychotic phenomena, often to the exclusion of other, equally troubling, presentations.

Mental health problems such as anxiety-related disorders are often left undiagnosed and untreated in people with psychosis at levels which would trigger intervention in those presenting solely with that condition.

While CBT became a widely practised and successful treatment for a variety of common mental health conditions; primarily depression and anxiety-related disorders, it took several decades before CBT was first advocated in the treatment of psychosis. Since the 1990s many researchers and clinicians have focused on understanding the origin, development and maintenance of positive psychotic symptoms and how best to treat these particular phenomena. CBT for psychosis drew on the principles and interventions developed for anxiety and depression and modified these to treat psychotic symptoms. CBT for schizophrenia is now widely accepted as an effective treatment in the reduction of psychotic symptoms. Indeed, a review of findings led the National Institute for Health and Clinical Excellence to recommend 'offer[ing] CBT to all people with schizophrenia. This can be started either during the acute phase or later including in in-patient settings' (NICE, 2010). There are now many excellent treatment manuals available which focus on the assessment and treatment of psychotic symptoms (Kingdon & Turkington, 2004; Fowler *et al*, 1995; Chadwick *et al*, 1996; Beck *et al*, 2009).

Interestingly, however, despite its roots in the treatment of emotional disorders and the success of CBT for schizophrenia, the treatment of co-occurring emotional disorders in people with psychosis has been largely ignored. This is slowly changing and this book hopes to provide a guide for clinicians treating clients with psychosis who also present with common mental health conditions. There is a growing realisation that services need to adopt an individual and holistic approach to the treatment of psychosis, not merely focus on positive symptoms. Instrumental in this change has been the recovery movement; a growing body of service users who advocate self-help, empowerment and the right to be treated as everyone else.

Psychosis is common; about one person in a hundred is likely to receive a diagnosis of schizophrenia in their lifetime and the same prevalence is found in bipolar disorder (BPS, 2000). Emotional disorders are even more common, eg with lifetime prevalence rates tending to vary between 2 and 3 per cent for obsessional compulsive disorder (OCD), 8 per cent for PTSD and 13 per cent for social anxiety disorder. Moreover, in those with psychosis, the presence of a co-occurring emotional disorder is significantly higher, eg a typical prevalence rate for OCD of 15.8 per cent found in a sample of 76 people with schizophrenia is seven times higher than chance (Kruger *et al*, 2000). Given these increased rates and the consequences of co-occurring emotional disorders for people with psychosis, development of treatment tailored to these problems is essential.

Similarly, as so succinctly described by Dyck *et al* (2000), negative symptoms are not the 'squeaky wheel' of schizophrenia and as such have not attracted as much investment in the development of psychological assessment and treatment as have positive symptoms. Although they have been implicated in a number of vital factors such as poor long-term prognosis, lower subjective quality of life and relapse, people with high levels of negative symptoms tend to receive the same input as those with few or no negative symptoms (Dyck *et al*, 2000). Although negative symptoms were often believed to be intractable and CBT for negative symptoms is a relatively recent development, a number of notable treatment successes have been established (eg Rector *et al*, 2003).

A distinction is often drawn between affective psychoses which involve clear mood components, for example schizoaffective disorder, and the non-affective psychoses, such as schizophrenia and delusional disorder, which are seen as unrelated to mood disturbance. However, problems of elevated and low mood also arise in people with schizophrenia and delusional disorders. Mood disorders are often subsumed by a diagnosis of psychosis rather than seen as separate co-morbid disorders. In people diagnosed with schizophrenia in particular, mood variation can often be overlooked if it is not the primary presenting problem. However, recent advances in CBT for bipolar disorder are now finding their way into the treatment of people with a range of psychotic presentations.

This book draws together advances in the understanding, assessment and treatment of stress, negative symptoms, social anxiety, OCD, PTSD and mood disturbance in people with a diagnosis of psychosis, to provide a practical guide for clinicians.

Chapter outlines

Chapter 1 focuses on the critical importance of stress in psychosis. Stress exerts a major influence on the development and maintenance of symptoms. The vulnerability-stress model (sometimes called the diathesis-stress model) (Zubin and Spring, 1977) of schizophrenia is central to the understanding of the range of factors implicated in the onset and maintenance of psychosis. Acute or prolonged stress causes activation of somatic and cognitive vulnerabilities to psychosis and, for example, can increase the salience of distorted thoughts. This chapter outlines the role of stress in psychosis, describes the assessment of stress and provides a working model of stress and psychosis. Interventions are described in detail including measures to minimise the stress of therapy and ways of responding positively to stress. Cognitive and behavioural techniques are detailed for the successful management of stress, as are methods for building resilience and interpersonal effectiveness.

Chapter 2 addresses the very significant and often overlooked group of difficulties known as negative symptoms; the emotional, motivational and behavioural deficits common in psychosis. This chapter describes the variety of negative symptoms and their importance; it details the assessment of negative symptoms and how to differentiate them from symptoms with similar presentations such as depression. A cognitive model of negative symptoms is presented and a guide to formulation is explained and illustrated by case example. Treatment of negative symptoms is described in detail with reference to a proposed treatment path from convalescence through active cognitive-behavioural treatment to lifestyle changes. Client information sheets on understanding negative symptoms and overcoming negative symptoms are provided.

Chapters 3, 4 and 5 address the most common anxiety-related disorders in psychosis: social anxiety disorder, obsessional compulsive disorder and post-traumatic stress disorder. Birchwood (2003) argued that because such disorders are so prevalent in psychosis they should be understood by their core pathway rather than merely in terms of diagnosis. He suggested three core, but not mutually exclusive, pathways: emotional disorder intrinsic to psychosis, emotional disorder as a psychological reaction to psychosis and emotional disorder and psychosis as the product of disturbed developmental pathways. These pathways are explored for each of the disorders with the intention of understanding the aetiology and maintenance of anxiety in psychosis in order to inform formulation and treatment.

Each of the three chapters examines the significance of the particular anxiety disorder for people with psychosis, describes assessment issues and tools and provides a CBT working model by which to understand the condition. A guide to formulation of each disorder in people with psychosis is presented together with case examples to illustrate formulation in action. Detailed cognitive and behavioural treatment interventions are described with particular emphasis on modifications, challenges and contra-indications for this client group. Client handouts explaining the disorders and their treatment are provided at the end of each chapter.

The final chapter focuses on mood disturbance in psychosis. Types of mood disorder are described and the significance of mood fluctuation in psychosis discussed. Assessment of mood disturbance is outlined with a number of different approaches explained. A working model based on the vulnerability-stress model modified for bipolar disorder is presented and formulation is described with reference to an illustrative case example. A treatment plan for clients with mood disturbance is described including strategies for enhancing motivation to change in those whose elevated moods are problematic but not necessarily distressing. Specific measures to stabilise sleep and behavioural patterns are described together with identification of prodromal signs and how to respond positively. Client handouts for understanding mood disturbance are provided.

How to use this book

It is hoped that this handbook will be valuable to clinicians who are familiar with CBT for psychotic symptoms but who want to help their clients to actively manage stress, negative symptoms, emotional and mood disorders.

It is recommended that clients with psychosis be routinely assessed in regard to stress and coping, and their experience of negative symptoms. They should also be screened for any difficulties with social anxiety, OCD, past traumas and mood fluctuations.

This is a practice guide which provides an understanding of each of the areas of difficulty, together with assessment tools, and a working model. Case conceptualisation is assisted by a guide to formulation and it is suggested that the models and case examples be used to assist individual formulation. The treatment sections detail specific interventions and suggested treatment pathways. Treatment is, of course, a collaborative venture and each step – from assessment through to formulation and treatment planning – should be made with the client. Education about the approach is provided in client information sheets which are intended to introduce the treatment approach. These are designed to be used as a handout to aid discussion and to encourage clients to ask questions and be active in developing their own treatment plans.

1 Stress and psychosis

Stress appears to have both a general and a specific effect on people with psychosis. In general, stress has a clear impact on both physical health and psychological well-being. It is implicated in the exacerbation of many medical conditions and diseases including coronary heart disease, stroke, stomach ulcers and heart attack (Powell and Enright, 1990). In addition, stress is commonly implicated in the development and maintenance of many psychological disorders including anxiety, depression, obsessive-compulsive disorder and phobia. Stress plays a specific critical role in psychosis, indeed Zubin and Spring's (1977) seminal 'vulnerability-stress model' of schizophrenia continues to inform research and clinical practice today. The model proposes that certain characteristics such as limited attentional capacity and hyper-autonomic arousal serve as vulnerability factors and that environmental and personal stressors can precipitate psychotic episodes in vulnerable individuals (Nuechterlein and Dawson, 1984). Individuals who have poor coping skills or inadequate coping resources might have an underlying vulnerability to the development of psychosis (Norman and Malla 1993). A comparison of people at very high risk of developing psychosis with a control group found that they were significantly more distressed by events, felt that they coped more poorly and used more emotion-oriented coping strategies than did the comparison group (Phillips *et al*, 2012). The authors suggest that preventative interventions should include treatment focusing on stress management and enhancing coping skills.

Assessment of stress

Stress can be measured and monitored in a number of ways. A formal measure of emotional distress can be helpful in gauging a client's current emotional state. A range of measures to assess stress, stressors and coping is available:

- *The Depression Anxiety Stress Scales* (DASS) (Lovibond and Lovibond, 1995) are a set of three self-report scales designed to measure the negative emotional states of depression, anxiety and stress. The stress scale is sensitive to levels of chronic non-specific arousal. It assesses difficulty relaxing, nervous arousal, and being easily upset or agitated, irritable or over-reactive and impatient. Clients use four-point severity-and-frequency scales to rate the extent to which they have experienced each state over the past week. The DASS is presented in the Appendix (*see* p. 146).

- *The Lifestyle Appraisal Questionnaire* (LAQ) (Craig *et al*, 1996) provides a comprehensive assessment of health and stress. It is an instrument designed to assess lifestyle from a multi-factorial perspective. It assesses cumulative risks and perceived stress of life. The questionnaire provides a sensitive measure of change with treated clients reporting a reduction in their cognitive appraisal of life stress (Craig *et al*, 1996).
- *Hassles scale* (Kanner *et al*, 1981) measures minor distressing events. This can be particularly useful as day-to-day stressors often have more impact than infrequent major life events (Malla and Norman, 1992). One hundred and seventeen potential irritants in the areas of work, health, family, friends, the environment, practical considerations and chance occurrences are listed. The client rates by severity (1–3) any item that occurred in the past month. The scale can be administered as a one-off measure of current hassles or completed over consecutive months to monitor stressors over time. Derived scores include frequency (number of items checked), cumulative severity (sum of the three-point rating scale) and intensity (cumulative severity divided by frequency), thus providing an index of how strongly or intensely the average hassle was experienced, regardless of the number of hassles checked.
- *Perceived Stress Scale* (Cohen *et al*, 1983) is a 14-item measure of the degree to which situations in one's life are appraised as stressful. It is designed to examine the role of non-specific appraised stress in the aetiology of disease and behavioural disorders and as an outcome measure of experienced levels of stress. General stress and perceived coping are measured.

Once a client has become proficient at recognising their stress levels, daily monitoring using a simple analogue scale can be helpful. Technical measurement is also possible; stress in 'real-world' daily functioning has been measured by experience sampling using palm computers to assess stress at various intervals during the day (Kimhy *et al*, 2010).

Working model of stress and psychosis

A working model of the role of stress in psychosis is presented in Figure 1.1. The model is informed by the vulnerability-stress model of schizophrenia (Zubin and Spring, 1977) together with models of stress in the general population proposed by Cooper (1981) its adaptation (Powell and Enright, 1990) and the work of Lazarus (1971) on stress and disease. Lazarus identifies three important components which are incorporated into the model of stress: 1) the notion of demands taxing a system, 2) the appraisal or perception of threat, and 3) the importance of the response of that system.

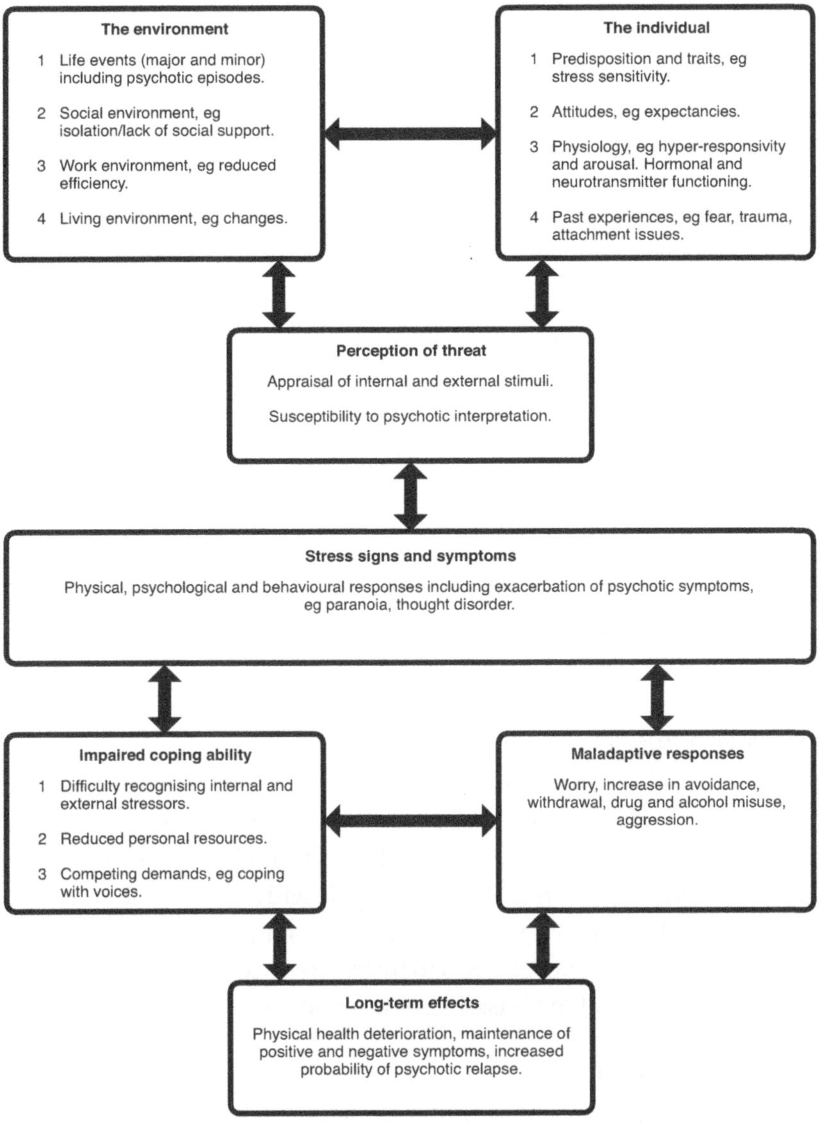

FIGURE 1.1 Working model of stress and psychosis

The environment

1) Life events

Life events which involve change – even positive change such as going on holiday or getting married – have been found to have significant effects on a person's susceptibility to stress-related health problems (Holmes and Rahe, 1967). An accumulation of life events is often found in the period leading up to a psychotic episode. It appears that people with psychosis have a lower threshold for experiencing stress; indeed the course of psychosis seems to be less influenced by relatively rare major life events and more by the build-up of more common minor life events (Malla and Norman, 1992).

In addition, the development of a psychotic illness is itself a very significant life event and commonly leads to other profound changes in relationships, living environment, work, education, financial situation, recreation and personal achievement.

2) Social environment

Social contact is important: it enables people to have fun; can provide alternative perspectives, distraction, opportunity to talk about difficulties and to receive information and help, and can reduce rumination and introspection. People with mental illness often have minimal social contact due to reduced social abilities, fear of social situations, stigma and discrimination or simply due to being unable to attend work or other social settings because of psychotic symptoms. Social isolation reduces a person's opportunities to express their feelings and to gain support from others. This not only increases stress but can also provide fertile ground for the development of paranoid or suspicious beliefs because opportunity to receive feedback from others, which can help to reduce the expansion of inaccurate appraisals, is limited.

3) Work environment

People commonly show deterioration in work performance in the period prior to developing acute psychotic symptoms. This frequently leads to increased stress due to attempts to work harder or longer hours to make up for lost efficiency. In the prodromal phase a person is likely to struggle with tasks which were previously manageable, find difficulty relating to colleagues, and fear being reprimanded or made redundant. The effect of stress is to further reduce performance and a vicious cycle of deterioration and increased stress can ensue.

4) Living environment

Psychosis often develops in early adulthood when people are becoming independent and moving out of the family home, sometimes to a different geographical location and usually coinciding with changes in social environment, employment or education. The experience of psychosis itself commonly results in changes in living environment such as moving back in with family, living in shared accommodation or hospitalisation. This brings with it increased stress due to loss of independence, noise, lack of privacy and the demands of other people. Alternatively, social isolation and having to fend for oneself can result in significant stress.

The individual

1) Predisposition and traits

There are a number of personality characteristics commonly found in children who go on to develop schizophrenia: they tend to be more introverted and withdrawn and prefer to spend time on their own rather than with others (Ellison *et al*, 1998). Traits such as a tendency to suspiciousness or making external attributions might also be considered both to predispose to psychosis and to create stress.

2) Attitudes

There appear to be some people who are 'stress resistant': they experience significant stress but seem to be unaffected by it. In a study of such individuals three factors were found to be important in maintaining this resilience to stress: a sense of control over situations and events, having a sense of purpose and commitment, and an ability to be flexible and to deal with ambiguity (Kobasa, 1982). People with psychosis frequently lack a sense of control in their lives, they can feel at the mercy of their symptoms and indeed often delusional beliefs develop around the feeling of literally being controlled by others. Avolition and lack of motivation are common negative symptoms which can manifest as lacking a sense of purpose. People with psychosis often struggle with ambiguity and tend to be concrete rather than flexible. Similarly, many have defeatist attitudes, are sensitive to perceived criticism and have low expectancies for pleasure or success (Beck *et al*, 2009). Thus, people with a predisposition to psychosis might be said to be stress-prone rather than stress-resistant.

3) Physiology

Genetic variability creates individual differences in physiological arousal in the general population. The autonomic nervous system which controls the body's response to stress appears to be more reactive in people who develop schizophrenia. Electrodermal over-activity can lead to hyper-responsivity and such individuals become more easily aroused to stressors (Zubin and Spring, 1977). Overactive dopamine systems together with other biological components might be important in the development of schizophrenia. It has been proposed that normal life stressors might cause exacerbations of hormonal (eg cortisol) activity and neurotransmitter responses, particularly dopamine. Positive symptoms might result from the increase in dopamine activity, whereas negative symptoms might be considered as adaptive responses to stress (Walker and Diforio, 1997).

4) Past experiences

Many people who go on to develop psychosis have experienced childhood trauma such as physical, sexual, emotional abuse and/or neglect (Read *et al*, 2005). Commonly they will have been raised in a family where one or both parents had mental health problems, and/or drug and alcohol abuse. Attachment problems are also a common feature in the histories of people with psychosis. These factors play a major role in later mental health and the ability to cope with stress.

Perception of threat

What one finds threatening and the degree of the perceived threat are dependent upon past experiences, knowledge, attitudes and beliefs. People who develop psychosis often experience common stimuli as potentially threatening, eg strangers. There is also a tendency to misinterpret neutral stimuli, eg an unintentional glance could be interpreted as having malevolent intent. Such individuals can become hyper-vigilant and sensitive to cues in the environment which might signal threat. Aberrant salience – the tendency to find significant meanings where there are none – is a common experience in people with psychosis, eg a person wearing a red coat might be interpreted as indicating a warning. Perceived threat is therefore very common in people with psychosis, and this is pivotal to the experience of stress.

The two-way arrows in Figure 1.1 indicate that the signs and symptoms of stress can themselves be misinterpreted and increase perceived threat. Misinterpretation of bodily sensations such as chest pains, palpitations or nausea can feed into delusional beliefs, eg of being poisoned or persecuted. People with psychosis commonly make external attributions of internal events (Beck *et al*, 2009).

Stress signs and symptoms

There are many physical, psychological and behavioural signs and symptoms of stress, including: palpitations, nausea, restlessness, inability to concentrate, irritability and insomnia.

If individuals misinterpret such signs as emanating from an external source, this can lead to distress and also to a strengthening of potentially delusional explanations such as delusions of control, paranoia or persecution, eg 'There is a devil inside me', 'I am being tormented'.

Difficulty concentrating, making decisions, forgetfulness and irrational ideas are all common psychological stress reactions found in the general population. In individuals with psychosis, positive and negative symptoms are likely to compound such stress symptoms.

Behavioural reactions to stress such as avoidance of anxiety-provoking situations and social withdrawal are also common reactions to stress and again can exacerbate such tendencies in people with psychosis.

Formal thought disorder can be viewed as part of a stress response to negative automatic thoughts elicited by various events. It has been suggested that the process is similar to that of stuttering, in that stressful situations exacerbate both types of symptoms and the phenomena can occur in anyone under certain traumatic conditions (Beck *et al*, 2009). Thought disorder tends to worsen in conditions of increased stress such as discussion of emotionally salient topics (Docherty *et al*, 2003).

The common signs and symptoms of stress are shown in client information sheet 1.1.

Impaired coping ability

Resilience to stress depends on the individual's ability to successfully cope with stressors. However, three factors commonly impair coping ability.

1) Difficulty accurately recognising internal and external stressors

Mood disturbance, preoccupation with delusional beliefs, distraction by voices and loss of volition all contribute to reducing the ability to make accurate judgements about matters such as the source and effects of stress. In addition, the tendency to make external attributions for internal events exacerbates distress.

2) Reduced personal resources to deal with stress

Often a person's resources are limited by the effects of negative symptoms, depressed mood or other consequences of psychotic symptoms. Commonly a person directs their energy to coping with the demands of positive symptoms such as voices and does not have resources to deal with additional stressors when they arise.

3) Imbalance between competing demands and personal resources

People with psychosis are often struggling with the demands of the illness – including taking anti-psychotic medication, attending medical appointments and struggling to cope with the psychosis itself.

Maladaptive responses

As with the general population, people with psychosis often develop maladaptive responses in an attempt to cope with stress. Typical responses include excessive worrying, avoidance, social withdrawal, drug and alcohol misuse and aggression.

Long-term effects

Over time, maladaptive coping strategies can become problematic, eg drug and alcohol dependence, development of anxiety disorder and other 'co-morbid' conditions. Long-term stress also has physical repercussions such as high blood pressure, heart disease and other stress-related illnesses. Residual psychotic symptoms can be maintained or exacerbated and indeed there is an increased risk of psychotic relapse in those experiencing high levels of stress (Nuechterlein and Dawson, 1984).

CLIENT INFORMATION SHEET 1.1 – SIGNS AND SYMPTOMS OF STRESS

Physical signs and symptoms

- Lethargy
- High blood pressure
- Tingling sensations
- Numbness
- Aches and pains
- Stomach ulcers
- Increased susceptibility to colds, mouth ulcers
- 'Butterflies' in stomach
- Nausea
- Palpitations
- Headaches, migraine
- Muscle tension
- Fast, shallow breathing
- Dizziness
- Feeling faint
- Diarrhoea
- Sweating
- Blushing
- Stress related illnesses, eg heart disease

Psychological signs and symptoms

- Muddled or racing thoughts
- Poor concentration
- Feeling tense or 'wound up'
- Worry, rumination
- Inability to relax, restlessness
- Difficulty making decisions
- Forgetfulness
- Negativity, pessimism
- Self-critical thoughts
- 'Obsessional' thoughts
- Increase in thinking errors

Behavioural signs and symptoms

- Avoidance of anxiety-provoking situations
- Reduced performance

- Increase in mistakes
- Difficulty in clear communication
- Aggression, hostility
- Crying
- Over-activity or under-activity
- Irritability
- Social withdrawal
- Increased use of alcohol, cigarettes, drugs
- Over-eating, under-eating
- Increase in obsessional tendencies
- Clumsiness
- Insomnia
- Loss of sexual interest
- Recklessness

Interventions for stress in psychosis

The multi-factorial working model of stress and psychosis presented suggests that treatment focusing on stress reduction and management would help to improve not only general well-being but also psychotic symptoms, and would reduce the risk of relapse. The model indicates many areas which are likely to be useful targets for intervention.

Therapy itself could be considered as potentially stressful. Box 1.1 lists a number of measures which might be employed to minimise such stress.

Psycho-education

Initial sessions focusing on orientating the client to the concept of stress and its potential role in their well-being can help to de-mystify stress and provide a framework for interventions. Three main areas can be addressed:

1) The role of stress in psychosis

Exploring the client's own experiences in relation to the working model helps to draw together many factors which might be relevant to their particular circumstances. The working model can serve as a template to understanding stress and psychosis interactions whilst also demonstrating that apparently disparate experiences are often linked, eg build-up of life events prior to an acute episode.

Box 1.1 Measures to minimise the stress of therapy

- Additional time and emphasis spent on helping the person feel comfortable can significantly reduce stress as can practical considerations such as providing tea and biscuits.
- Agree on the optimum length of sessions; shorter sessions are usually preferable.
- Consider the frequency of sessions; weekly or twice-weekly meetings might help to desensitise the person to such contact and aid memory. Long periods between sessions can make every session feel like the first.
- A relaxed and informal style will help put the client at ease.
- Consider the number of people present; the presence of a trainee or other professional not normally present can feel threatening. Sometimes a relative or friend can provide support, or might increase tension.
- Where appropriate a less formal setting than an interview room can help to normalise the interaction.
- Focus on stress reduction and coping before addressing emotionally salient topics.
- Note any exacerbation in thought disorder or other overt signs of stress in order to identify what triggers stress, eg discussion of particular person or subject; what psychological meaning does the person ascribe to such triggers?

2) The signs and symptoms of stress

Education about the variety of signs and symptoms of stress and how to recognise them can be very reassuring. Often clients can misattribute symptoms of stress and can develop erroneous or sometimes delusional explanations for symptoms, eg believing that one is being physically manipulated or punished. Client information sheet 1.1 lists the common physical, psychological and behavioural signs and symptoms of stress.

3) Identification of stressors

Life is stressful and often stress is so insidious that it is not recognised, thus it can gradually build up and become problematic. Awareness of specific stressors is necessary to enable one to cope more effectively with the stressor. It is difficult to address 'general stress' but once stressors are identified they become much easier to deal with. Client information sheet 1.2 'Identification of stressors' can be used to focus discussion and elicit information to help the client to understand and contextualise their experiences.

CLIENT INFORMATION SHEET 1.2 – IDENTIFICATION OF STRESSORS

Life events (Major)

Have you experienced any of the following in the past 12 months?

- Personal illness
- Personal accident
- Hospitalisation
- Illness or accident of close relative or friend
- Death of close relative or friend
- Divorce or separation from partner
- Divorce of parents or siblings
- Change in employment
- Marriage
- Moved house or change in accommodation
- Imprisonment or arrest
- Legal problems
- Pregnancy and birth of a child
- Significant change in financial situation

Life events (Minor)

Consider events that occur in daily life which can be stressful, and which might have occurred in the past month.

- Argument with friend
- Cold/influenza
- Acquired new pet
- Problem with household management, eg plumbing
- Illness of friend or pet
- Problem with budgeting
- Change in recreational activity
- 'Paperwork' issue, eg insurance claim
- Holiday period, eg Easter, Christmas
- Stopped smoking/drinking
- Medical/dental/other treatment
- Car/transport problem
- Increase/decrease in responsibility
- Rent arrears or debts

Social environment

Social relationships can be a great source of support; however, some social contacts can also be stressors. Try to identify who, why and when social contacts become stressful.

Who?

- Family members
- Friends
- Professionals
- Colleagues
- Religious, other social community
- Neighbours
- Housemates

Why?

- Critical
- Over-protective
- Controlling
- Uncaring
- Demanding
- Unsupportive
- Argumentative
- Over-emotional
- Inconsiderate

When?

- Disagreement
- Particular issues, eg financial
- Specific behaviours, eg making noise

Work environment

Is your work environment a source of stress? If so, try to identify specific stressors.

- Anti-social hours, long hours
- Lack of clarity of role
- Work overload
- Work under-load
- Work conditions, eg sharing desk/office
- Specific colleagues
- Boss
- Travel to and from work
- Feeling under-valued

Living environment

Are there specific sources of stress in your living environment?

- Lack of privacy
- Noise
- Living with others
- Living alone
- Size of accommodation
- Location
- Neighbours

Personal factors

Do you have any particular things which upset or irritate you? It is helpful to identify any such 'sensitivities'. Often they are quite individual. Here are some examples:

- Having to wait
- People coughing/sneezing
- People talking about drugs
- Whispering
- Untidiness
- Bad driving
- Queuing
- People laughing
- Breaking rules

Internal stressors are those that we create for ourselves by the way we think and behave. Do any of these apply to you?

- Time urgency, eg always having to be punctual
- Being self-critical
- Being too concerned about my appearance
- Excessive worrying about minor problems
- Being too concerned about what others might think
- Trying to compete constantly with others
- Wanting approval/praise/attention from others
- Thinking that the worst is going to happen
- Putting excessive demands on myself

Responding positively to stress

Fortunately, there are many ways to cope effectively with stressors and to build resilience to stress. Once the client has identified their own stressors and is familiar with their personal physical, psychological and behavioural manifestations, sessions can focus on how to manage stress effectively (Williams, 2004). Coping can be enhanced by addressing three key areas.

1) Problem solving

Having identified specific stressors, explore with the client whether anything can be done to change the situation which is creating stress. Often simple solutions become apparent once particular problems are clarified, eg if the person is stressed by sharing an office with someone with whom they do not get along, asking to change office might solve the problem. Less easily solved problems require a more systematic approach. A seven-step problem-solving strategy and worked example is described in Chapter 2, 'Negative symptoms'.

2) Lifestyle balance

The model proposes that stress is created by demands taxing a system. Reducing demands to a manageable level would allow the system to achieve greater balance. Lifestyle, in this context, includes:

- Activities of daily living such as shopping, cooking, laundry
- Chores, eg filling in forms, paying bills, servicing the car
- Pleasures, eg hobbies and interests
- Self-care, ie diet, exercise, sleep
- Structure, ie how one divides one's time between various activities such as leisure activities, work, education, socialising.

Imbalance in any of these areas can affect the others and lead to stress, for example lack of sleep might affect performance and ability to function during the day. This could result in the postponement of necessary chores leading to a build-up of tasks which become too daunting to undertake. Depressed or anxious thoughts might develop and cause further sleep disturbance.

Discussion of the person's lifestyle is likely to reveal areas where balance might be restored. This might include techniques such as:

- prioritising important tasks
- seeking help
- distributing chores and pleasures evenly throughout the week
- simplifying tasks such as doing weekly rather than daily shopping
- building in rewards for achievements or completion of avoided chores.

Attitude towards 'chores' can also be addressed and modified to make them more pleasurable, eg vacuuming can be viewed as a tedious activity but by playing music and viewing it as a 'work-out' session it can become a pleasure. Discussion of diet, sleep pattern and exercise can reveal potential areas for goal planning and positive change. Scheduling in time to rest, relax and engage in pleasurable activity at least once per day can significantly reduce stress.

3) Coping with life events

Flexible response to change contributes greatly to one's ability to cope with stress. Attitude to change is important; often people who are stress-prone tend to view change negatively and have a 'why me?' attitude, whereas more stress-resistant people view change as an inevitable part of life.

Often life events are predictable: leaving home, moving house, taking a new job, getting married, retirement. Anticipating and preparing for such events can help to reduce their impact. Reducing other demands during this period can also be helpful. Where possible, changing one thing at a time can be less stressful than making a number of life changes. For example, if starting a new job it might be better not to plan on moving house or taking on other new projects for at least six months.

Unpredictable life events can also be managed to reduce their impact. Awareness that any change requires a period of adjustment and adaptation can help to relieve pressure on oneself and from others. Traumatic life events such as bereavement might be coped with by seeking help from others, joining a support group or finding out about typical reactions, ie 'what is normal?' Bereavement has recognised stages and the effects can continue for months or years.

Cognition and cognitive techniques

> *Tension is who you think you should be. Relaxation is who you are.*
>
> Chinese proverb

Thinking plays a major role in the development and maintenance of stress. The experience of stress is primarily self-generated. It emanates from one's

- appraisals of situations – 'I won't get the job'
- attributions – 'He is deliberately trying to upset me'
- distorted or irrational thinking – 'My future is bleak because no one will ever want to be with me.'

In addition to these commonly experienced cognitions, people with psychosis can also experience significant stress caused by misattributions inherent in positive symptoms such as paranoid ideation, persecutory beliefs, and other delusional ideation: 'I am being watched', 'my family are imposters', 'they are trying to torture me because I know too much', 'I caused that plane to crash'. Derogatory or negative auditory hallucinations often cause extreme stress. If one's 'self-talk' anticipating failure can create significant stress, how much more compelling are externally attributed voices telling the person that they will fail. Similarly, negative symptoms, such as avolition, which generate strong defeatist beliefs and negative expectancies for success or pleasure can create significant associated stress.

Successful cognitive behavioural therapy for delusions and hallucinations is likely to have a significant impact on stress generated by these symptoms. The three techniques described below for the treatment of cognitions which exacerbate stress can also help to reduce the general distress associated with psychotic symptoms.

Self-instructional training (SIT)

SIT was developed by Meichenbaum (1975) who described how what we say to ourselves, known as 'self-talk', can influence our moods and behaviour. Negative self-talk can lead to stress and anxiety and can create self-fulfilling prophesies of failure. SIT therefore aims to help the person to talk to themselves in a confident, positive way which anticipates success.

Self-instructional training

1. Identify typical self talk. Person monitors self-statements made before, during and following a task.
2. Develop alternative self-statements which would promote confidence and chances of success. Statements should include those which anticipate the task, those to be used during the task itself and those for use immediately following the task. Include self-praise.
3. Practise the use of self-talk. This can be rehearsed during the session prior to testing out 'in vivo'.
4. Self-statements can be written on cue cards while the person practises and becomes more comfortable with the new approach.

SIT example

Billie became stressed when going to see her psychiatrist. Monitoring self-talk produced the following cognitions:

- Anticipating the visit – 'I won't be able to answer his questions', 'I won't remember what to tell him'.
- During the visit – 'He thinks I'm stupid and I'm wasting his time', 'I want to leave, when will this be over?'

- Following the visit – 'I'm glad that is over, it was awful, I hate doing this, I'm such an idiot'.

Self-talk, alternative statements:

> Anticipatory – 'This will be fine', 'I've seen him before and he knows I get nervous', 'I can ask if I don't know what he means', 'I can make a note of things I want to tell him'.
>
> During – 'I have every right to be here', 'He is listening to what I am saying', 'I am using this time well'.
>
> Following – 'Well done, I did it!', 'I did really well', 'It was good to talk'.

Cognitive restructuring

This technique was developed in the 1970s (eg Beck, 1976) and has become a standard CBT tool. It involves helping the client to identify the negative automatic thoughts they experience in relation to specific situations, which create psychological symptoms, eg of depression, anxiety, stress. Clients are encouraged to record these thoughts, together with the situation and a quantitative rating of the symptom. The client can then be guided to restructure the thought by asking specific questions, such as

- 'What is the evidence for this thought?'
- 'Are there any alternative explanations?'
- 'How likely is it?'
- 'So what if it happens?'

The client is thus guided towards answers which help to challenge their negative automatic thoughts and to replace such thoughts with more rational explanations. The alternative explanations can be written down in the 'double-column' technique.

Example

Henry became stressed when he could hear his neighbours through the adjoining wall. He recorded his negative automatic thoughts at these times:

> 'They are really noisy. I can't stand living here since they moved in. They are doing it deliberately to wind me up. They want me to move out. I might end up hitting them and get arrested. I will end up homeless.'

Stress rating = 10

Henry realised how his negative automatic thoughts spiralled, each one leading to an even more irrational negative thought. The alternative explanations were helpful in putting the stressor in perspective and reducing the stress experienced.

Negative automatic thought	Alternative explanation
They are really noisy.	The walls are very thin. They can hear me as well.
I can't stand living here since they moved in.	There are lots of good things about my flat; I like where I am living 90 per cent of the time.
They are doing it deliberately to wind me up.	Most of the noise is just from things everyone does, eg running a shower, vacuuming, watching TV.
They want me to move out.	They seem very friendly when we meet. They fixed my TV aerial because I don't have a ladder.
I might end up hitting them and get arrested.	I have never hit anyone in my life.
I will end up homeless.	I know I won't this is just where my mind goes when I am really stressed.

Henry was able to challenge his negative automatic thoughts when he heard noises from his neighbours. Stress rating = 3.

'Hot-spot' recognition

Enabling the client to recognise familiar cognitions which tend to elicit a stress response can be helpful. Such recognition can be used to signal the need to challenge the thought in order to reduce the impact. Prepared action can then be taken every time the thought occurs.

Typical 'hot' cognitions might include those closely linked to the perception of threat – physical or psychological – and those related to sensitivity to criticism, suspiciousness, personalising and projection of blame. For example, 'People are whispering about me', 'She looked at me as if I was rubbish', 'He wants me to fail', 'I will mess this up', 'They are against me'.

Cognitive challenges can be rehearsed in session, written on cue cards and used every time the thought occurs. These are some real cognitive responses that clients have successfully employed:

> 'There's that thought again.'
> 'It's only a thought, not a fact.'
> 'Maybe yes maybe no, I don't know.'
> 'Hot-spot; just cool it down!'

Building resilience

It appears that psychological resistance to stress might be greatly influenced by one's approach to life. Possessing a sense of control, a sense of purpose and flexibility tends to enable people to view changes as opportunities rather than as problems.

Building resilience might therefore be possible by exploring the client's attitude to life:

- Do you feel in control of your life?
- Can you influence situations or events?
- Do you believe in fate?
- Do you feel that you have many choices in life?
- Are you able to solve problems?
- Are the things that happen to you 'other people's fault'?

The extent to which people feel that events are contingent on their own behaviour rather than controlled externally is likely to impact upon their ability to take control of their life. If a client has a high external 'locus of control', exploring where these beliefs originated and designing tasks to test the view can be helpful. Of course the person's appraisal might be realistic especially if they experience episodes of hospitalisation or have difficulty managing their own affairs. However, any opportunity to take charge of one's own life and direction in recreation, family and social life can help to build self-confidence and resilience. Attempts to shift perspective to a more internal sense of control can lead to increased self-efficacy and self-empowerment.

Similarly, having a sense of purpose can help a person to focus on what is important to that individual rather than to become side-tracked by distractions and irritations. Goal setting and problem solving are particularly useful if these enable a person to recognise and address important cognitions and attitudes which might hinder success.

Opportunities to develop flexibility of thought and action can also build resilience. Recognising old habits and deliberately doing things differently can be liberating. For example, a person might be encouraged to try something which they had previous thought was 'not me'. This could be a simple and small change such as wearing something different from their usual style. Larger changes such as 'acting opposite' in a situation which they have identified as being stressful and unproductive can be rehearsed in session.

Physical and mental relaxation

Awareness of the physical and mental signals that the body produces when stressed is not automatic – it needs to be cultivated. Stress is often so much a part of our daily lives that it continues and even accumulates unnoticed. Sensitivity to these signs can be improved by learning to notice the contrast between tension and relaxation. Individuals often 'store up' tension in particular areas of the body: shoulders, neck, lower back. Noticing this tension can then act as a cue to releasing the strain by deliberately relaxing the muscles, changing posture and/or using breathing techniques.

There are several relaxation techniques.

Progressive Muscular Relaxation (PMR)

This method can be used to develop sensitivity to tense muscles and contrast this with the sensations associated with physical relaxation. It can be done sitting or lying down, whichever the client finds most comfortable. The person is instructed to deliberately tense, hold and relax each muscle group in turn. Starting with the hand clenched into a fist, followed by the forearm, and each upper arm in turn, before moving down the body through forehead, face, neck, shoulders, chest, back, abdomen to the legs and the feet. PMR exercises are readily available on compact disc for people to practise between sessions until they have learnt the routine. Once this has been successfully accomplished, clients can practise just noticing the state of tension or relaxation of each muscle group, without tensing. If they notice tension they are instructed to try to allow the muscle to relax, if it will; trying too hard to relax can, paradoxically, produce tension. Daily practice is recommended. Eventually the person will become adept at noticing areas of tension and consciously relaxing the body in response.

PMR has been found to effectively alleviate anxiety in people with schizophrenia (Chen *et al*, 2009).

Diaphragmatic breathing

This deep-breathing technique can help to focus the mind on one's breathing and to relax the muscles. Instructions:

- Sit with your back straight but not tense, or lie down on your back with arms and legs outstretched.
- Put one hand gently on your stomach.
- Inhale naturally and slowly through your nose, this will slow down the intake of breath.
- Focus your mind on your belly and notice how it rises naturally as you inhale.
- Slowly exhale through your nose to regulate the release of air while noticing the belly fall.
- Continue for several repetitions try to allow the breath to 'breathe itself'.

Guided imagery

Relaxation through guided imagery can be very effective in reducing stress. The success of this method appears to be related to the person's imagery ability: the greater the ability the greater is the shift towards comfortable emotional states and the displacement of stress (Watanabe *et al*, 2006).

Many guided imagery scripts are available in print or on CD. Such scripts give detailed descriptions of, for example, being in a tropical garden, walking in a forest, sitting in the mountains or by a river.

Body scan meditation

A particularly successful method by which to cultivate a profound sense of physical and mental relaxation is the guided body scan meditation. This meditation has been popularised and developed by Jon Kabat-Zinn, as part of his Mindfulness Based Stress Reduction (MBSR) programme at the University of Massachusetts Medical Centre. The participant is guided through each part of the body in turn, starting with the toes of the left foot and visiting each body part to the top of the head. The person breathes into and out from each body part and if any tension is noted it is allowed to release on the out breath. Mental relaxation is also cultivated by noticing when the mind wanders away from the body, noting where it has gone, and bringing it back to focus on the body part. Daily practice of meditation has been shown to benefit people with a variety of physical and psychological problems. A full account of the MBSR programme can be found in the book *Full Catastrophe Living* (Kabat-Zinn, 1990). Mindfulness tapes and CDs are also available.

Assertiveness

To deal effectively with stressors, assertive interactions with other people are often required. People with psychosis often find it difficult to assert themselves; this is likely to be due to a number of factors including pre-existing personality variables such as a tendency to introversion, the experiences of psychotic symptoms which can cause alienation from others, social withdrawal, loss of confidence, and experiences of stigma and discrimination.

Rights that are often taken for granted – the right to express one's opinions and beliefs, to be 'oneself', to be listened to and taken seriously, to be illogical in making decisions, to set one's own priorities – are frequently removed from people with psychosis. Unfortunately, all too often clients report that decisions that affect them – at home, work or concerning their care and treatment – have been made without their having been consulted.

The underlying philosophy of assertiveness training is that everyone has the same basic human rights. Assertiveness is the ability to stand up for one's rights without violating the rights of others. Assertiveness is a social skill which can be learned, and training often covers areas such as:

1. recognising one's own passive and/or aggressive behaviour and its consequences
2. how to deal with difficult interactions, eg refusing requests
3. expressing legitimate anger
4. dealing with criticism
5. negotiation
6. resolution of grievances.

There is a substantial literature on assertiveness both for use by mental health professionals and for those seeking self-help, which can assist in planning sessions (Powell, 2010; Hadfield and Hasson, 2010). Practising the skills and rehearsing personally relevant scenarios are central to developing successful interactions. Scenarios might include: a job interview, asking one's psychiatrist for a medication review, making an important purchase.

2 Negative symptoms

Definition and description

Negative symptoms are characterised by the absence of behaviours or experiences that would normally be expected within a person's social context. They are essentially emotional, motivational and behavioural deficits. Negative symptomatology is outlined in Table 2.1.

TABLE 2.1 Negative symptomatology: the five As

Symptom	Definition	Manifestation
Avolition	Lack of energy, drive and interest.	Neglect of personal care, lack of motivation, apathy, negligible physical energy. Loss of sense of purpose.
Anhedonia	Loss of interest, inability to experience pleasure.	Relinquishment of hobbies, limited recreation.
Asociality	Lack of involvement in social relationships.	Loss of interest in intimacy, reduced participation in relationships, active withdrawal from social interaction.
Affective blunting	Impoverishment of emotional expression, reactivity and feeling.	Little change in facial expression, monotonous voice, limited spontaneous movements/gestures. Reduced range and intensity of both positive and negative emotions.
Alogia	Impoverishment of thinking and speech.	Limited quantity of spontaneous speech and/or speech lacking in content, loss of train of thought, increased time taken to respond.

Formal diagnosis of negative symptoms is described in the Diagnostic and Statistical Manual (DSM-IV-TR) (American Psychiatric Association 2000) and International Classification of Diseases (ICD-10) (World Health Organization 1992) as requiring at least two key symptoms for a period of one month and evidence of symptoms causing substantial interference with work, education, family, or self-care with disturbance over a period of at least six months.

The importance of negative symptoms

The importance of negative symptoms is often overlooked due to the focus upon the more overt positive symptoms of psychosis. Negative symptoms are not the 'squeaky wheel' of schizophrenia (Dyck *et al*, 2000). Despite the enormous social and personal consequences of negative symptoms, researchers found that people with high levels of negative symptoms did not receive any more outpatient service hours than did those who had low levels (Dyck *et al*, 2000).

Negative symptoms have been found to be associated with a variety of significant issues:

Poor long-term prognosis

Schizophrenia with many negative symptoms has been found to be associated with poor premorbid functioning, insidious onset, partial or no remissions during the initial years of illness and, in most cases, a progressive course leading to permanent disability. Having fewer negative symptoms, on the other hand, was associated with good premorbid functioning, acute onset, intermittent early course and a better prognosis. Indeed, negative symptoms appear to be better predictors of differential illness history, course and long-term functional capacity than are positive symptoms (Fenton and McGlashan, 1991). These researchers also found that two negative symptoms in particular – anhedonia and affective flattening – contribute most significantly to poor outcome.

Reduced social and occupational functioning

The nature of negative symptoms, particularly social withdrawal and loss of motivation can lead to loss of social contact, loss of employment and resultant further loss of functioning. People with prominent negative symptoms were found to have poorer performance on task orientation, social skills and personal presentation during a work programme than those without prominent negative symptoms (Lysaker and Bell, 1995).

Lower subjective quality of life

Psychological treatment often focuses upon reducing the impact of positive symptoms with the aim of improving quality of life. However, subjective quality of life, as measured by asking people how they feel about their lives in general (Lehman, 1988) was found to be more influenced by negative rather than positive symptoms (Packer *et al*, 1997).

Relapse

Dyck *et al* (2000) found that negative symptoms were significantly correlated with relapse to acute illness. The precise relationship between negative symptoms and relapse remains unclear.

People with negative symptoms can often appear less able to benefit from psychosocial interventions due to their difficulty with motivation and the effort required to engage in such interactions.

Research into expressed emotion in relatives of people with psychosis has found that in the two years following discharge from hospital patients from high-expressed-emotion homes had a significantly greater relapse rate than those from low-expressed-emotion homes (Leff and Vaughn, 1981). Avolition and social withdrawal can have an enormous impact upon the relatives, friends and carers of people with psychosis who can become frustrated and aggrieved at the apparent lack of interest from the person they are trying to help. It can be argued that this in turn can lead to increased 'expressed emotion', blame and criticism, which might increase stress and the likelihood of psychotic relapse. Negative symptoms contribute to carer burden and to family conflict which predicts poor prognostic outcomes (Perlick *et al*, 2006; Weisman *et al*, 2000).

Primary and secondary negative symptoms

It is possible to group deficits into three constellations: primary negative symptoms, secondary negative symptoms and related symptoms. Related symptoms include those which are often confused with negative symptoms but have a different aetiology. These types of negative symptoms are described in more detail in Box 2.1.

Box 2.1 Primary and secondary negative symptoms

Primary negative symptoms are those which result directly from the psychosis. They are usually persistent and stable over time although some people experience changes in the intensity of their primary symptoms. The term 'deficit syndrome' is often used to describe this pattern of core negative symptoms. It has been proposed (Carpenter *et al*, 1988) that specific criteria should be met to describe the deficit form of schizophrenia: it is defined by the presence of at least two negative symptoms – restricted affect, diminished emotional range, poverty of speech with curbing of interest and decrease in curiosity, diminished sense of purpose, or reduced social drive for a period of 12 months. The symptoms should always be present during periods of clinical stability or during recovery from psychotic exacerbation (Carpenter *et al*, 1988).

Secondary negative symptoms are those which arise indirectly as a function of the positive symptoms of psychosis, the environment, including environmental deprivation, anxiety, depression, stressful life events, etc. These symptoms tend to show more fluctuation and tend to be less enduring (Carpenter *et al*, 1988).

People can, of course, experience both deficit syndrome and secondary negative symptoms, as well as related symptoms, and the three categories should be seen as interrelated rather than entirely separate.

Related symptoms: when a negative symptom is not a negative symptom

When a person has a diagnosis of a mental illness there is sometimes a tendency to view any deficit or loss of functioning as a negative symptom. However, there are several other potential reasons for a decline in functioning, loss of motivation, social withdrawal and other behaviours that are not directly attributable to the process of the illness.

Side effects of antipsychotic medication

Sometimes medication side effects are referred to as secondary negative symptoms; however, it is more accurate to locate the effects, such as sedation and loss of volition, to their source – the medication – rather than to the illness. Indeed, clients often complain that the medication is making them worse; they feel 'slowed up' or 'like a zombie'. If this is dismissed as a negative symptom, rather than listened to and acted upon, it can be detrimental to the therapeutic relationship and ultimately to compliance.

A commonly reported unwanted side effect of anti-psychotic medication is sedation. Whilst sometimes this effect is helpful in improving ability to sleep and reducing agitation, often people complain of loss of motivation, drowsiness and lethargy. If sedation is problematic, the prescriber might consider changing the dose or the regime, eg splitting the dose or taking it in the evening rather than in the morning can often help. Sometimes small reductions in dose can be accompanied by significant benefits in reduced lethargy. If the person remains significantly affected, trying an alternative medication might be indicated.

Depression

Depression is a disorder of mood or affect which often manifests in physical symptoms such as sleep disturbance, reduced appetite and corresponding weight loss or increased appetite and weight gain, together with characteristic changes in thinking about oneself, one's world and one's future. Severity varies from mild to severe; in which case the person might feel total despair, remain in bed and have frequent thoughts of suicide. People with a diagnosis of schizophrenia commonly feel helpless and hopeless, experience low mood and indeed might be at risk of developing depression. Often psychosis is seen as the explanation for all of a person's symptoms and depression can be overlooked. If a person with a diagnosis of schizophrenia has flat affect, lacks motivation, stops socialising and spends a great deal of time in bed they might be depressed; negative symptoms should not be assumed. Diurnal variation, where people tend to feel worse in the morning and relatively better in the afternoon can be characteristic of depression but some depressed people experience unremitting low mood throughout the day and some people with schizophrenia can experience diurnal variation due to medication side effects. Negative attitudes towards social interaction have been found to be more stable in people with schizophrenia than in those with depression (Blanchard *et al*, 2001).

Post-traumatic stress disorder (PTSD)

Estimated prevalence of co-morbid schizophrenia and PTSD generally varies between 20 and 40 per cent (Bebbington *et al*, 2004). It is therefore likely that approximately one in three patients with schizophrenia would meet the diagnostic criteria for PTSD. Commonly PTSD in this group remains unrecognised as once a diagnosis of schizophrenia is reached, many of the symptoms of PTSD are assumed to be psychotic. The relationship between trauma and psychosis is significant and several studies have found increased rates of sexual abuse, physical abuse and bullying in the histories of people who go on to develop psychosis (Bebbington *et al*, 2004). Indeed, there also appears to be a direct relationship between severity of abuse and severity of psychosis (Janssen *et al*, 2004).

There are a number of phenomenological links between PTSD symptoms and psychotic symptoms. War veterans with PTSD and psychotic symptoms had similar positive and negative psychotic symptom scores to those with schizophrenia (Hamner *et al*, 2000). PTSD symptoms include emotional numbing, social isolation and impaired concentration. Typically, avoidance is used in a bid to manage the occurrence of intrusive images and flashbacks. Sleep disturbance is also common in both PTSD and psychosis and in itself can lead to further loss of functioning and lethargy. PTSD and psychosis is the subject of Chapter 5.

Cognitive deficits

There appears to be an overlap between cognitive deficits – which are usually defined in terms of performance on various tasks such as memory, concentration and problem solving – and negative symptoms. The true relationship between them is further compromised as several negative symptom assessment measures include cognitive deficit items, eg the *Scale for the Assessment of Negative Symptoms* (SANS) (Andreasen, 1984) includes items on attention including attentiveness during mental status testing. Although it is possible that cognitive deficits and negative symptoms are both different manifestations of the same basic underlying process, recent evidence suggests that they are more likely to have separate aetiologies (Harvey *et al*, 2006). Therefore treatments that target cognitive deficits are not likely to have a significant impact on negative symptoms and vice versa. Assessment of a client's functional impairments should examine the reasons underlying them, eg is the person unable to work because of inability to concentrate or due to lack of motivation?

It has also been suggested that defeatist beliefs might act as a mediator of cognitive impairments, negative symptoms and functioning in schizophrenia. This has useful practical implications in that tackling defeatist beliefs directly would be likely to improve functioning (Grant and Beck, 2009).

Assessment

The type of assessment undertaken is dependent on the reason for referral and the presenting problems identified. Assessment can be broken down into five phases; it is not always appropriate to employ all and sometimes a good interview is sufficient.

1) Screening for symptoms masquerading as negative symptoms

Medication side effects

The presence of lethargy is the main indicator of possible sedative effects of medication. Review the onset and course of the lethargy and match this against the medication regimen and dosage changes. If there is a clear link between the medication and sedative side effects, then possible options should be discussed with the prescriber. Monitor closely any change in perceived lethargy with dosage/regimen changes. Blunted affect and akinesia might also signal possible medication effects.

Depression

It is usually helpful to screen for depression even in the absence of classic indicators such as changes in sleep and appetite, which can be unaffected. A widely used tool specifically developed for the assessment of the level of depression in schizophrenia is the *Calgary Depression Scale* (Addington *et al*, 1993). Further information can be found in Chapter 6 'Mood disturbance in psychosis'. The scale is presented in the Appendix (*see* p. 148).

In addition, monitoring of mood using a simple 10-point scale at designated times in the morning, afternoon and evening can help to establish any diurnal variation. The stability of negative attitudes towards socialising or social affiliation might also provide evidence to help in discriminating between depression and negative symptoms.

Post-traumatic stress disorder (PTSD)

Given the prevalence of sexual abuse, physical abuse and bullying, it is recommended that all patients be routinely screened for exposure to childhood and adult trauma. Post-traumatic stress disorder is commonly undetected in this client group. In addition to taking a personal history of experience of abuse and other traumatic events, explore the person's psychological response to psychotic symptoms. In particular, be alert to emotional numbing, avoidance, impaired concentration, sleep disturbance, intrusive images, repetitive dreams and flashbacks. If PTSD is suspected, use of a formal screening measure such as the *PTSD Checklist* (PCL-S) is indicated (Weathers *et al*, 1991). More in-depth evaluation can be carried out using the *Clinician-Administered PTSD Scale for Schizophrenia* (CAPS-S) (Gearon *et al*, 2004). *See* Chapter 5, 'Post-traumatic stress disorder and psychosis'.

Cognitive deficits

These can be assessed using specific cognitive functioning tests to measure abilities such as memory, concentration and problem solving. Patients with a diagnosis of schizophrenia have been found to show impairments upon a very wide range of different cognitive tasks. The most significant deficits have been suggested to be: poor information processing speed; poor new learning capabilities and executive function deficits such as limited problem-solving abilities; difficulty in the organisation of new material; poor 'dual' tasking; and limited response control. If conducting a neuropsychological assessment it is also worth taking into consideration the tasks in which people with psychosis are generally not impaired. These include those with more circumscribed and concrete demands, those which involve the use of well-learned early skills such as reading and those which are repetitive.

2) Client and/or carer interview for problem identification including discriminating between primary and secondary negative symptoms

Careful questioning covering the range of negative symptoms, including onset, course, stability, duration and severity, will enable identification of those symptoms which might be most amenable to treatment and those which are most troubling to the client, and will help to distinguish between primary and secondary symptoms. Careful recording of responses is useful as triggers, cognitive distortions and underlying beliefs are often revealed in such detailed discussion and are good material for future treatment targets. If the client is unable to provide the information due to memory or concentration difficulties or poverty of speech, carer interviews can be very helpful. A checklist to aid such interviews is provided in Box 2.2. If conducting research, a formal assessment tool, the *Schedule for the Deficit Syndrome* (SDS) (Kirkpatrick *et al*, 1989), is an instrument for categorising clients with schizophrenia into those with and those without the deficit syndrome. Each of six negative symptoms is scored on a five-point scale (normal to severely impaired) on the basis of an interview.

Box 2.2 Checklist for interview assessment of negative symptoms

- Attempt to distinguish between primary and secondary negative symptoms, eg what course do they follow? Check for stability and/or fluctuation, presence even during periods of remission in positive symptoms, and longevity.
  - **Specifically explore:**
    —Restricted affect
    —Diminished emotional range
    —Poverty of speech
    —Curbing of interests
    —Diminished sense of purpose
    —Reduced social drive
- What function do the symptoms serve?
  - **Social withdrawal:**
    —a coping response to fear (secondary to paranoia)
    —avoidance of acute distress (social anxiety)
    —lack of enjoyment of or desire for relationships (schizoid personality)
    —negative expectancies (depression)
    —lethargy (medication side effects)
  - **Poverty of speech:**
    —Lack of thoughts (psychotic process)
    —Difficulty communicating/word finding (anxiety)
    —Fear of criticism/ridicule (social anxiety)
    —Helplessness/hopelessness (depression)
    —Preoccupation/interference by voices/distress beliefs (positive symptoms)
- Do the symptoms have trait-like characteristics suggesting continuity with premorbid personality?
- What relationship do they have with positive symptoms?
  - Persistent and independent?
  - Elevations following onset of paranoia/voices?
  - Explore thoughts, feelings and behaviour in response to all voices and delusional beliefs.

3) Formal measures of negative symptoms

There are several scales designed to measure negative symptoms. In a study of eight rating scales used to retrospectively assess patients with schizophrenia, the reliability of all scales was fair to good and there were high positive correlations between the scales when used to rate negative symptoms dimensionally (Fenton and McGlashan, 1992).

The Scale for the Assessment of Negative Symptoms (SANS) (Andreasen, 1981)

This is an observational rating scale which covers five categories of negative symptoms: alogia, affective flattening, avolition-apathy, anhedonia-asociality and attention. Administration takes approximately 10–20 minutes. It can be used to measure change over time. It is the sister of the *Scale for the Assessment of Positive Symptoms* (SAPS).

The Positive and Negative Syndrome Scale (PANSS) (Kay et al*, 1987)*

This rates a variety of symptoms by interview which takes approximately 30–40 minutes, together with observation. The negative symptom items include blunted affect, emotional withdrawal, lack of spontaneity and stereotyped thinking. The negative symptoms are well defined and include severity ratings which make it sensitive to change.

The Clinical Assessment Interview for Negative Symptoms (CAINS) (Blanchard et al*, 2011).*

In response to the National Institute for Mental Health-Measurement and Treatment Research to Improve Cognition in Schizophrenia (NIMH-MATRICS) consensus statement on negative symptoms (Kirkpatrick *et al*, 2006) a multi-site study is in the process of constructing a 'next-generation' negative symptom scale, the *Clinical Assessment Interview for Negative Symptoms* (CAINS) (Blanchard *et al*, 2011). It is hoped that this will be a major advance in the formal assessment, and subsequent treatment, of negative symptoms.

Additional measures to consider include measures of the client's own *subjective* experience. These can help to highlight those symptoms which are most troubling to the client and thus, as well as producing important information, can reinforce collaboration and enhance the therapeutic relationship.

The Subjective Experience of Negative Symptoms Scale (SENSS) (Selten et al*, 1993)*

This is an interview-based rating scale designed to measure several aspects of the subjective experience of negative symptoms such as awareness, causal attribution, disruption, distress. The item set is derived from the SANS allowing a comparison of subjective and 'objective' ratings. Discrepancies can be used as a measure of awareness of negative symptoms.

The Subjective Deficit Syndrome Scale (SDSS) (Jaeger et al, *1990)*

This is a 19-item scale which measures self-reported complaints and covers irritability, motivation, mood, indecisiveness, sleep and anhedonia. Interestingly, the developers of the scale found that it correlated with global measures of psychopathology in acute but not chronic clients and did not correlate with negative symptoms or medication side effects.

Assessment of premorbid function can be helpful in determining the extent of deficits which are likely to be attributable to the consequences of the diagnosis, help to identify the emergence of negative symptoms and contextualise specific deficits.

The Premorbid Adjustment Scale (PAS) (Cannon-Spoor et al, *1982)*

This covers sociability, withdrawal, peer relationships, scholastic performance, establishment of independence, social-personal adjustment, degree of interest in life and energy level.

A measure of social performance might also be considered when exploring the effects of negative symptoms on functioning in particular environments and situations.

The Social Behaviour Schedule (SBS) (Wing and Brown, 1970)

This is a rating scale for specific problem behaviours such as hygiene, initiating conversation, communication, socialisation, concentration, activity level, occupation, leisure. It is designed primarily for use with people with long-term contact with mental health services.

4) Additional assessment as suggested by formulation, eg negative appraisals, social affiliation

Fear of Negative Evaluation Scale (FNE) (Watson and Friend, 1969)

This is a 30-item true/false scale designed to measure the degree to which people experience apprehension at the prospect of being evaluated negatively. There is also a 12-item version which correlates highly (.96) with the original scale (Leary, 1983).

Revised Social Anhedonia Scale (RSAS) (Eckblad et al, *1982) and Revised Physical Anhedonia Scale (RPAS) (Chapman and Chapman, 1978)*

Anhedonia can be assessed with the revised versions of the social and physical anhedonia scales. These true/false self-report measures provide indices of the pleasure derived from physical and social-interpersonal sources, respectively. They have been shown to be reliable, with internal consistency reliabilities (coefficient a) of 0.79 to 0.82 for the RPAS (Chapman *et al*, 1982) and 0.79 for the RSAS (Mishlove and Chapman, 1985).

The Inventory of Interpersonal Problems (IIP) (Horowitz et al, *1988)*

This inventory consists of 127 items measuring difficulties relating to other people. There are six subscales: assertive, sociable, submissive, intimate, responsible and controlling. Each item is rated on a five-point scale. A short 32-item version is also available (Barkham *et al*, 1996).

5) Ongoing monitoring of symptoms

Personal questionnaires can be constructed with the client in order to track changes in the target symptom(s) over an appropriate period, eg daily, weekly or monthly monitoring. The most appropriate monitoring frequency can be determined by the type of problem identified. Symptoms that are more consistent, such as loss of motivation, can be sampled less often, whereas those which are most changeable, eg loss of pleasure, can be monitored more frequently. A simple 10-point scale can be used to rate level of difficulty in specific areas – the more clearly defined the problem the easier it will be to monitor. Examples might include: difficulty showing emotions, not knowing what to say during a conversation or not wanting to socialise.

Cognitive model of negative symptoms

The cognitive conceptualisation of negative symptoms has been advanced in recent years by Beck, Rector and others (Rector *et al*, 2005; Beck *et al*, 2009). They propose that specific cognitive appraisals and beliefs play a role in the maintenance and persistence of negative symptoms. The model is based upon the vulnerability-stress model proposed in a seminal paper in the 1970s and still widely influential (Zubin and Spring, 1977). The key tenet is that as a result of a range of genetic and environmental factors, some people become susceptible to developing negative symptoms. Beck *et al* (2005) propose that some people possess predispositional schizoid traits which influence the development of negative symptoms. Negative social and performance attitudes become incorporated into these traits. Low expectancies for pleasure or success reinforce the expression and maintenance of negative symptoms. Beck *et al* (2005) suggest that 'negative symptoms represent, in part, a compensatory pattern of disengagement in response to threatening delusional beliefs, perceived social threat and anticipated failure in tasks and social activities'. Thus, according to the model, negative symptoms are, to a degree, coping behaviours. For example, a person who experiences persecutory delusions might stay away from other people because they evoke fear which might manifest in the negative symptom of asociality. Further, patients' perceptions of their own limited resources can lead them to minimise investment in activities that require effort (Rector *et al*, 2005).

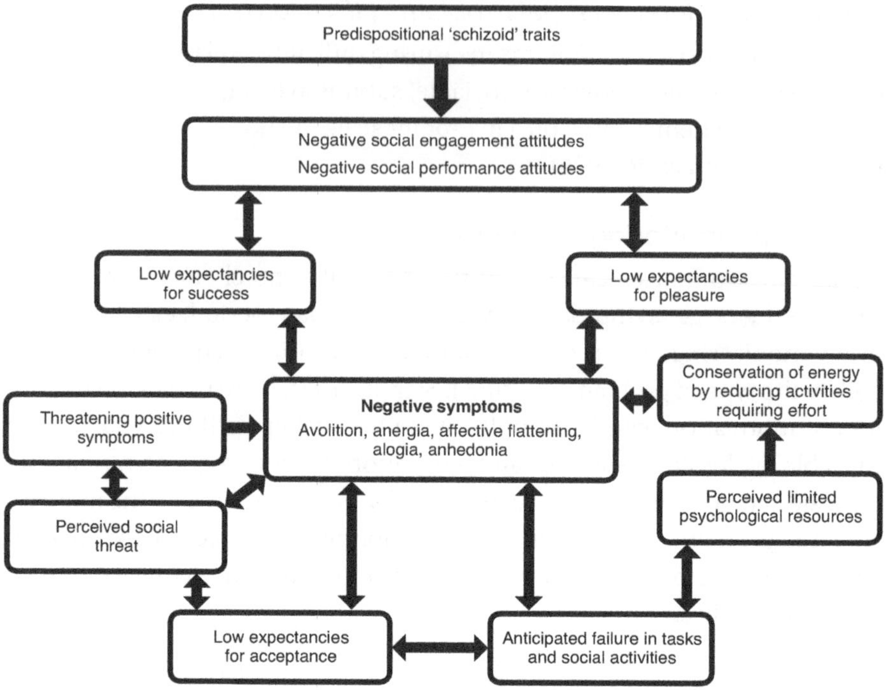

FIGURE 2.1 Cognitive model of negative symptoms (adapted from Rector *et al* (2005))

Formulation

The assessment phase will have produced valuable information with which to develop a formulation. This bringing together of the important elements in the development and maintenance of the symptoms is a vital component of treatment and helps the client to make sense of their experiences in context.

The formulation can be based upon the cognitive model described in Figure 2.1, on a broader vulnerability-stress formulation or on any modification which best fits the individual.

A key part of the formulation is coming to an understanding of the function of the negative symptoms. There are two major types: first those directly related to positive symptoms. These can function as the person's coping strategies aimed at reducing threats from voices or beliefs, and/or behaviour related to the delusional beliefs. Examples would include staying in bed to avoid triggering of voices, reducing contact with family and friends due to paranoid beliefs, or avoiding conversation due to the interference from voices. The second type is negative symptoms unrelated to positive symptoms, primarily those of avolition, loss of motivation and emotional disengagement. Treatment strategies will be determined by the formulation so a full understanding of the symptoms and their role is vital prior to treatment.

CASE VIGNETTE: EMILE

Emile is a 24-year-old man of Lebanese origin. His parents moved to the UK as refugees when he was six years old and they lived in a deprived area of South London. His parents spoke only Arabic and he struggled to learn English or to find a peer group. As he grew up he remained on the periphery of social groups and was unable to find supportive friendships or to feel comfortable outside of his home. His parents were vigilant to possible negative influences such as drugs and crime and instilled a tendency to wariness, mistrust and worry. Emile struggled at school and had to retake a year, further alienating him from his peers. He was bullied and teased which reinforced his belief that he was different from others, that he was inadequate and could never 'fit it'. He failed to achieve any qualifications and left school at age 16 to work at his father's bakery. He had minimal social contact during the day and rarely went out in the evenings except to visit family with his parents. His work performance, which had initially been good gradually deteriorated, he was increasingly late

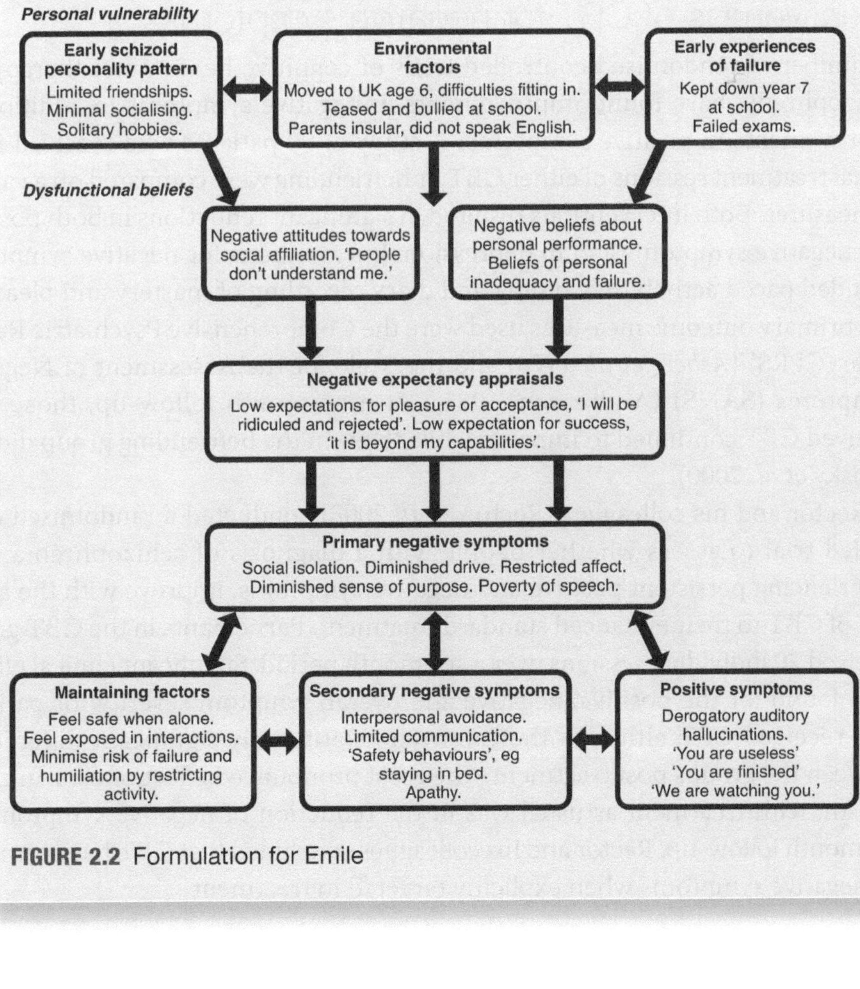

FIGURE 2.2 Formulation for Emile

and went home early, and following an argument with his father he refused to go to work. He rarely spoke to anyone and refused to leave the house. He believed that he was under 'special agent' surveillance and kept the curtains permanently closed. He heard derogatory voices telling him he was useless and commenting on his actions. Emile was diagnosed with paranoid schizophrenia when he was 19 years old. Whilst his paranoid beliefs responded to medication he continued to experience significant negative symptoms.

An example of a formulation for Emile is shown in Figure 2.2.

The formulation indicates areas for treatment focus. In Emile's case, addressing maintaining factors by gradual systematic exposure to perceived threats, tackling 'safety behaviours' and dysfunctional beliefs by cognitive therapy techniques and building low-stress social interactions was successful in reducing his negative symptoms.

Effectiveness of CBT for negative symptoms

A number of randomised controlled trials of cognitive behavioural therapy for schizophrenia have found improvements in negative symptoms in addition to improvements in positive symptoms. A study of 90 patients who received individual treatment sessions of either CBT or befriending were compared on a variety of measures. Both interventions resulted in significant reductions in both positive and negative symptoms and in depression. Interventions for negative symptoms included paced activity scheduling and diary recording of mastery and pleasure. The primary outcome measures used were the Comprehensive Psychiatric Rating Scale (CPRS) (*Asberg et al*, 1978) and the Scale for the Assessment of Negative Symptoms (SANS) (Andreasen, 1981). At nine-month follow-up, those who received CBT continued to improve while those in the befriending group did not (Sensky *et al*, 2000).

Rector and his colleagues (Rector *et al*, 2003) conducted a randomised controlled trial to assess whether people with a diagnosis of schizophrenia, and experiencing persistent positive and negative symptoms, improve with the addition of CBT to their enhanced standard treatment. Participants in the CBT group received 20 individual sessions over a six-month period. Significant clinical effects were found for the positive, negative and overall symptom severity for patients who received CBT although there were no statistically significant differences between the groups post treatment. The most pronounced effect of CBT in comparison with treatment as usual was in the reduction of negative symptoms at six-month follow-up. Rector and his colleagues concluded that CBT has an impact on negative symptoms when explicitly targeted in treatment.

Treatment

First motivate yourself!

The very thought of interventions with people with significant negative symptoms can be demoralising; clients can appear to be uninterested in or incapable of change, dispirited or resistant. We have all experienced the occasional 'heart-sink' moment when faced with a client with seemingly intransigent symptoms. The treatment of negative symptoms can feel like an uphill struggle. However, it does not have to be like this; there are four things to bear in mind to help to keep you motivated:

- This is a taste of what it feels like to have negative symptoms.
- Negative symptoms are amenable to change.
- The rewards are worth the investment, for both you and for the client.
- Your attitude and outlook are vital in communicating hope to the client.

Treatment planning

The type of treatment approach will be determined by the formulation. Those negative symptoms that are directly related to positive symptoms, ie avoidance strategies and a range of safety behaviours, can be significantly reduced by treatment of positive symptoms. If the negative symptoms arise from delusional beliefs they should be addressed within a cognitive behavioural framework for delusions. Similarly, CBT for auditory hallucinations is likely to reduce the need for withdrawal and avoidance coping strategies. If residual negative symptoms persist beyond successful CBT for positive symptoms, additional interventions such as in vivo exposure using graded hierarchies to overcome avoidance and safety behaviours are indicated.

The treatment of negative symptoms unrelated to positive symptoms is primarily concerned with improving interpersonal and emotional engagement and enhancing motivation. This requires a different treatment approach which is described in the remainder of this chapter. A suggested treatment path is shown in Figure 2.3.

Convalescence

Recovery from any serious condition involves a period of rest and recuperation. Interestingly, those recovering from serious psychiatric conditions are often urged to do the opposite, ie to engage in additional activities, to get out more and to push themselves. Kingdon and Turkington (2005) have been influential in proposing that people with schizophrenia should be enabled to 'recover in their own good time at their own pace'. They give the analogy of a broken leg which needs rest, protection and time to heal. Premature removal of the plaster cast or not immobilising the leg causes delayed healing or complications in the future. This is a useful concept to use with clients and carers and can be a great relief and reassurance.

Reducing demands and 'giving permission' to do less can help the person to feel validated, understood and can relieve the guilt which can accompany inactivity.

Paradoxically, suggesting that the person does less, and monitoring mood, during a period of fixed inactivity, eg staying in bed, can in itself lead to the desire to increase activity once the person feels that they have the resources to do so.

In their analysis of recovery, based on interviews with clients, Andresen *et al* (2006) suggest that the first stage is 'moratorium' – a time of withdrawal

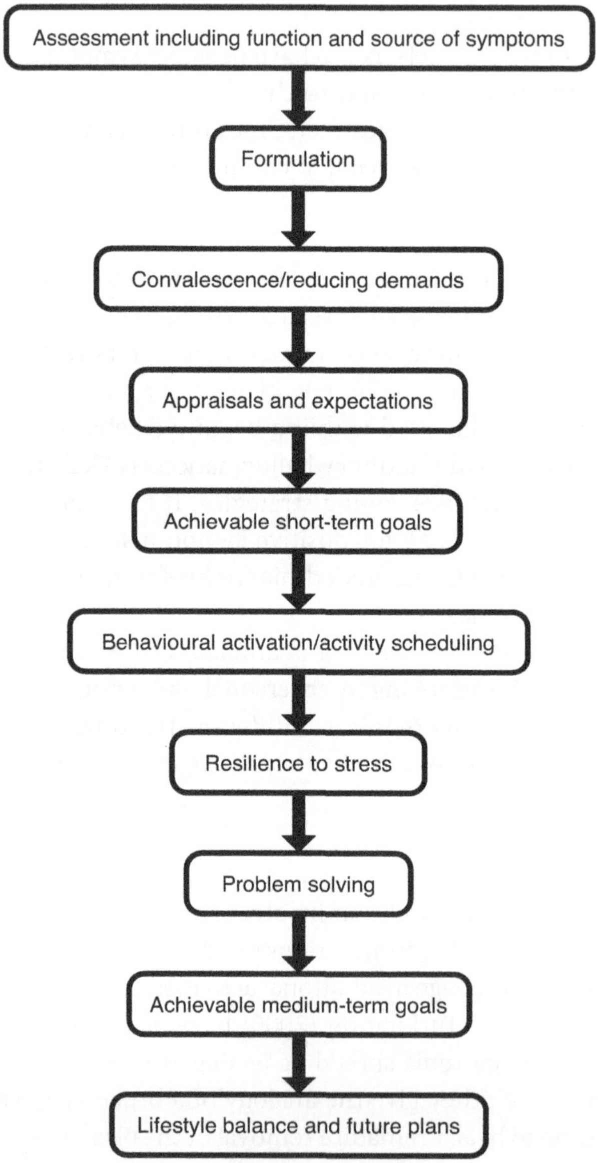

FIGURE 2.3 Flow diagram of suggested treatment path

characterised by a profound sense of loss and hopelessness – followed by 'awareness' – realisation that all is not lost and that a fulfilling life is possible.

Appraisals and expectations

> *Between the great things we cannot do and the small things we will not do, the danger is that we shall do nothing.*
>
> Adolph Monod

Building an understanding of the person's key appraisals and expectations leads to a fuller understanding of what particular attitudes and opinions they hold which are likely to maintain or to exacerbate their negative symptoms. Common appraisals have been described by Beck *et al* (2009), and these are listed in Box 2.3.

Box 2.3 Common appraisals and expectations in negative symptoms

Defeatist social expectations:
I will not be able to hold conversations.
People will reject or humiliate me.
I cannot cope with everyday interactions.
I will be criticised.

Defeatist performance beliefs:
I can't do the things I used to.
I lost my job therefore I'm a failure.
If you can't do things well there is no point in trying.
I have lost my skills.

Low expectations for pleasure:
I won't enjoy it.
Nothing gives me pleasure anymore.
It's all too much effort.
There is nothing to look forward to.

Low expectations for success:
I'm not good enough.
It will not work out for me.
I have given up my ambitions.
I'll never get a job.

Low expectations due to stigma:
People with schizophrenia cannot live a normal life.
Mental illness takes away all your chances.
I can't expect much now I have this condition.
I'm not a person anymore I'm a schizophrenic.

Perception of limited resources:
All my energy goes to fighting the symptoms.
Everything takes enormous effort.
I need to rest or my illness will get worse.
I have no strength.

A balance between the distortions of negative appraisal and unrealistically high expectations must also be found, ie the person's actual capabilities must be identified; low expectations are a psychological impediment only if they are inaccurate. Unrealistic goals and targets, whether stemming from the individual or from others – including mental health professionals – can create unnecessary pressure and be counterproductive.

Negative appraisals and expectancies: treatment

1) All-or-nothing thinking

Impairments might indeed have reduced a person's abilities; however one's cognitive responses to any deterioration can increase or decrease its impact. Explore all-or-nothing thinking which is characterised by beliefs such as 'If I can't get a job I can't do anything'.

2) Permanence

Just because something is the case at the present time does not mean that it will always be so. If a person is struggling with voices or delusional beliefs they are probably less able to take on additional tasks or might find it difficult to fulfil current responsibilities. However, capabilities change. Explore whether the person is over-generalising from 'worst-case' situations or assumes that things will always be this way. People often under-estimate their potential to change, to learn and to develop new interests. Hope and optimism are vital ingredients to change.

3) Non-acceptance

Wishing the illness had not happened, dwelling on 'what might have been' and becoming enmeshed in the damage the illness has caused are understandable reactions, but ultimately destructive. Acceptance of the way things are now, rather than ruminating on what has been lost, can mitigate against unfavourable comparisons between the past and present. Acceptance of the reality of the present is the first step to empowerment and hope for the future.

4) Negative anticipation

It is easy to put oneself off doing something by imagining it will be difficult, not enjoyable or unsuccessful. Negative anticipation can have a significant impact on motivation and prevent a person from even attempting something which they think will yield nothing positive. Gauging the accuracy of such predictions by rating anticipated and actual enjoyment or success or difficulty can demonstrate the effect of negative anticipation.

5) Negative self-perception

Negative self-statements such as 'I can't . . .' 'I'm just . . .' 'I won't be able to . . .' become self-fulfilling prophesies. Objective examination of such statements often reveals that such self-judgements are inaccurate and have been biased by negative assumptions.

6) Resignation

The trauma of experiencing a psychotic episode, the loss of relationships and occupational and other aspirations is often catastrophic. However resignation to 'this is the way my life is' can lead the person to giving up the pursuance of even small, easily achievable goals and the unnecessary long-term reliance on others for basic care. Dependence is sometimes necessary during periods of illness but long-term independence may very well be an achievable goal.

7) Conservation of resources

Doing less can be helpful during convalescence or in times of acute stress or illness; in the longer term, the less one does the less one wants to do. Often people hold erroneous beliefs that they need to conserve energy or they will become exhausted and that doing less, or returning to bed for long periods will help. Indeed, usually the opposite is the case; doing little increases tiredness and depletes energy whereas energy can be increased by gradual expansion of activities.

8) Social withdrawal

When a person feels unable to cope with social interaction or frequently uses avoidance and social withdrawal as ways of coping with symptoms, the solution can itself become a problem. Social withdrawal leads to social isolation, loneliness and erosion of confidence. Exploring ways of reducing social withdrawal and using it sparingly rather than as a 'default' position can prevent it becoming entrenched.

9) Defeatist beliefs

Defeatist beliefs such as 'I will never amount to anything' or 'It is not worth trying I can't succeed' lead to apathy, avoidance and passivity. Learning to challenge such beliefs can lead to improvements in mood as well as impacting on negative symptoms.

10) Stigma and negative views of mental illness

Many people, including those with mental health problems, hold negative views about mental illness and often believe myths such as it is not possible to get better, there is no treatment, it requires long-term hospitalisation. Exploring the concept of recovery and examining the person's own potential for recovery greatly assists in instilling hope and optimism.

Achievable short-term goals

Seventy percent of success in life is showing up.

Woody Allen

Recovery from psychosis is a gradual process which should proceed at the person's own pace while any associated pressure is minimised. Setting short-term goals is a good way of reducing the pressure to pursue long-term goals such as employment, marriage and independent accommodation, which might seem daunting and unattainable.

There are five key points in setting short-term goals:

1. They are short-term goals! That is, they are achievable in less than six months.
2. The goals are mutually agreed and client-led. The therapist assists in structuring the goals and helping to define the parameters.
3. Ensure they are easy to achieve and not likely to create pressure. The goal must be within, or below, the client's current capabilities.
4. Goals should be as specific as possible. Defining the goal is necessary so that it is clear what is to be achieved. 'Read more' is too general and difficult to measure whereas 'Join the library and read three books in three months', perhaps even specifying the books, clarifies the task and the time period.
5. Review the goal after an agreed time period. If the goal was achieved celebrate the success; if it was not, explore the reasons and re-set a more achievable goal.

Behavioural activation and activity scheduling

Behavioural activation is a structured intervention which focuses on helping people to re-establish daily routines, increase pleasurable activities and enhance motivation and engagement. The approach was originally devised for the treatment of depression and translates well to the treatment of negative symptoms.

Behavioural activation can evoke changes in three domains; cognitive, emotional and behavioural. Within the cognitive domain, clients can revise the way that they think about their capabilities and their ability to derive pleasure from life. Such interventions provide evidence with which to challenge defeatist beliefs such as 'nothing works' or 'I'm a failure'. Emotional changes can occur by improvements in the person's daily experiences, sense of achievement, pleasure and quality of life. Behavioural changes include increasing an individual's repertoire of activities and enhancing the pursuit of meaningful tasks. As we have seen, clients with negative symptoms frequently have low expectations for pleasure and success. Treatment that explicitly targets such beliefs and uses the feedback to change these expectations can be particularly helpful in maintaining motivation and engagement in the longer term (Beck *et al*, 2009).

Activity scheduling is designed together with the client to maximise their engagement with activities that they have chosen, increase their motivation and improve their quality of life. A seven-step procedure for activity scheduling is presented in Box 2.4.

Box 2.4 The seven steps of activity scheduling

Step 1

Together with the client, compile a list of activities from which they are likely to derive a sense of achievement and/or pleasure. These might include activities which they used to pursue but no longer engage in, those connected to previous or current general interests, or activities which are available locally, etc. Should discussion fail to provide any options, examination of a comprehensive list of possible activities can stimulate ideas. Such a list is presented in Table 2.2.

Step 2

Choose one activity and discuss how this can be incorporated into their week. This might raise distorted thoughts about the likelihood of pleasure or success.

Step 3

Discuss the concepts of anticipatory pleasure – namely that which one predicts, one will derive – and consummatory pleasure – namely, that which is actually experienced at the time. Explain that it is common to have thoughts which are negatively biased prior to engaging in an activity, especially a new one or one that the person has not undertaken for some time. Normalise this experience by common examples, eg going to the gym, mowing the lawn. The accuracy of such thoughts can be gauged by recording anticipatory and consummatory pleasure.

Step 4

Discuss any practical considerations or potential obstacles and schedule the activity to be carried out prior to the next session.

Step 5

Agree on and provide a simple rating scale to be completed prior to and immediately following the activity to record anticipated and actual experience of mastery and pleasure, eg 1–5 scale or percentage. The rating should be completed immediately following the activity as there is also a tendency to retrospectively minimise the pleasure experienced.

Step 6

Discuss the experience at the following session, particularly any discrepancies between anticipatory and consummatory pleasure. Identify and discuss any thinking errors such as all-or-nothing thinking, negative biases, and self-criticism. Focus on any thoughts which threaten motivation or engagement, eg guilt at failing to reach a self-imposed/previously achieved standard.

Step 7

Congratulate and encourage. Discuss and schedule in activity for following week; additional activities can be added when appropriate.

TABLE 2.2 Pleasurable activities

Painting/drawing/art	Horse riding
Card games	Fishing
Chess	Go to library
Gardening	Social event
Walking/rambling	Day trip
Jogging	Get a takeaway meal
Reading	Go out for a meal
Playing instrument	Pampering; hairdressers, manicure, etc.
Singing/choir	Spending time with pets
Sewing/knitting/embroidery	Swimming
Attending sporting event	DIY
Meeting up with a friend	Going to theatre or cinema
Cookery	Shopping
Concert	Collecting, eg fossils, stamps

Resilience to stress

People with psychosis are particularly vulnerable to stress due to a variety of biochemical, physiological, personality, genetic and social factors. Stress often plays a major role in psychotic relapse and in maintaining both positive and negative symptoms. Indeed, it has been proposed that in people vulnerable to schizophrenia, normal life stressors can cause exacerbations of abnormal hormonal and neurotransmitter responses, and that negative symptoms are an adaptive response to reduce stress (Walker and Diforio, 1997). It is therefore important to incorporate interventions to help to recognise and manage stress in all clients with psychosis. It is also important to ensure that treatment targets and interventions are not themselves experienced as additional pressure. Building resilience to stress is commonly identified as a treatment goal. Understanding and managing stress in clients with psychosis is described in Chapter 1.

Problem solving

Negative symptoms such as avolition can often create further problems which are perpetuated by inaction and avoidance. This vicious cycle then leads to further reduction in motivation and negative expectancies for success. Taking a positive view of such difficulties as problems which can be solved is ultimately empowering and can help to alleviate negative symptoms by instilling a sense of agency and control over one's life. The key to successful problem solving, particularly for people experiencing negative symptoms, is to break the problem down into easily manageable steps and to follow a simple strategy to assist in rational thinking and which leads directly to action.

The seven-step problem-solving strategy is presented in client information sheet 2.1.

CLIENT INFORMATION SHEET 2.1 THE SEVEN-STEP PROBLEM-SOLVING STRATEGY

Following these seven steps will help you to become an effective problem solver.

Step 1: Define the problem

Sometimes we need to decide exactly what the real problem is before we attempt to solve it. A problem can be defined by knowing what the situation is and what you would like it to be. Try asking yourself, 'Where am I with this and where would I like to be?' Don't necessarily believe your first answer! Ask yourself, 'Is this really the case?'

Step 2: Stop and think

Acting on our emotions generally leads to poor outcomes; for example, if we are driven by strong feelings of anger, resentment or rage it is likely that our actions will be aggressive and unhelpful. Usually emotional responding makes situations worse, not better. Thinking through problems before making decisions helps us to take the right actions. Taking all the information into account and reflecting on it stops us from behaving impulsively. Problems rarely need to be solved immediately so take your time and plan your responses. Think about what information you might need, what other people think and what alternatives there might be.

Step 3: Gather information

To make good decisions we need to gather accurate information and as much as possible.

Ask yourself, 'Who will give me the best information?' This person is not necessarily your best friend as they might be biased in your favour and not know all the facts. The best sources of information are expert and independent.

Step 4: Generate alternatives

Try to generate as many alternatives as possible; at this stage don't rule out any ideas. Be creative, ask other people what they would do, use 'brainstorming' – ie just write a list of alternatives.

Step 5: Think about the consequences

All solutions have the potential to have positive as well as negative consequences. Choose your top two alternatives from your list of options and do a 'cost-benefit' chart on each. This will help you to consider both the short-term and long-term costs and benefits. Often it will become clear which is the best option. If neither seems satisfactory, choose another option or go back to Step 4 and gather more information.

Step 6: Planning

Before carrying out your decision plan how to do this most effectively. You might want to consider, for example, whom to talk to, what to say, when to do it, etc.

Step 7: Action

Carry out your plan and see if it works. If it does, congratulate yourself. If it does not, go back to Step 4, 3, 2 or even 1 and try again.

In teaching the seven-step problem-solving approach, a worked example can be helpful to show the client how the system works in practice before going on to examine their own identified problem. A worked example is presented in Box 2.5.

Box 2.5 Problem solving example: lack of privacy at home

Anna is 23 years old and lives with her parents and two younger half-sisters aged 12 and 13 years. She feels that she rarely has any 'personal space' and although she has her own room she lacks privacy.

Step 1: Define the problem

Anna initially defined the problem as 'the house is too small for the family'. She then jumped to the solution that they need to move to a larger house or alternatively she should move out. However, when she asked herself, 'Where am I with this and where do I want to be?' she realised that the real problem was 'I am constantly pestered by family members and I want to have more uninterrupted time on my own'.

Step 2: Stop and think

At first Anna felt annoyed and wanted to just tell her family to stop harassing her and to keep out of her way. She realised that she had actually said this many times before to no effect. She needed to think about what her family thought and to seek advice from other people.

Step 3: Gather information

Anna decided to talk to her Community Psychiatric Nurse (CPN) and seek her advice. She also asked a person who also lived with their parents how they coped with intrusions.

Step 4: Generate alternatives

The alternatives Anna drew up were: go out more, save up and buy a caravan for the garden, put a lock on my door and don't answer when they knock, get a small cooker and fridge for my room and be more self-sufficient, agree 'ground rules' to create more uninterrupted time, create a 'quiet zone' in the house (currently a junk room) where no talking is allowed.

Step 5: Think about the consequences

Anna's top options were: agree 'ground rules' and create a 'quiet zone'.

- *Benefits of option one*: Everyone will have 'signed up' to the agreement, I will have the comfort of my own room, if I have time to myself I will feel more able to socialise with my family at other times.
- *Costs of option one*: The family might not stick to the rules and that would cause arguments.
- *Benefits of option two*: It will free up more space in the house, it would be easy for people to remember the purpose of the room.

- *Costs of option two*: Someone else might be in the room when I want to be alone, I won't be able to decorate it in my style because it's for everyone, and I will have to clear out the junk.

Step 6: Planning

Anna decided that option one would be best. She planned to raise the idea over dinner when everyone was together and there would be time to discuss it. She would ask each person their opinion, whether they thought the plan was fair and what obstacles there might be to sticking to the plan. To remind people that she should not be interrupted at agreed times she could hang a notice on her door.

Step 7: Action

Anna spoke to her family as planned. Her father had not realised that she felt that way; her stepmother had wanted to include her in the family and had been deliberately seeking her out to ask her opinion on things; her half-sisters had mainly wanted to borrow items or get advice, eg about make-up. They agreed that she would be available for an hour before the evening meal but would like her own space afterwards. All agreed to the plan. Success!

Achievable medium-term goals

> *To avoid criticism, do nothing, say nothing, be nothing.*
>
> Elbert Hubbard

Medium-term goals will emerge over time, as optimism and confidence increase. These ideas might include educational, occupational, social and recreational goals. The therapist's role is to focus on thoughts which might inhibit the goals. These commonly include sensitivity to criticism; self-doubt; fear of negative evaluation; shame at potentially failing to meet one's own, or others', expectations. Another constellation of thoughts which interfere with such goals are those which relate to the establishment of goals which are both realistic and meaningful: if a person has held high ambitions in the past, 'lesser' goals might hold no meaning. Alternatively, holding over ambitious goals such as studying medicine at Oxford can interfere with planning more realistic and achievable goals. Helping the client to set achievable medium-term goals is essentially a cognitive therapy task. CBT techniques such as Mastery/Pleasure ratings, activity scheduling, thought diaries and weekly progress logs can all be employed in the promotion of achieving goals. Beck *et al*

(2009) describe a five-stage process: 1) socialise the patient to the importance of setting goals; 2) break down broader goals into small, manageable steps; 3) structure and schedule the steps to be completed; 4) deal with barriers to engagement; and 5) negotiate setbacks.

Lifestyle balance and future plans

Homeostasis is the biological principle that the internal body attempts to remain in a state of balance and has a tendency towards stable conditions. As the external conditions vary, the body makes corrections to enable it to function optimally. This principle can be extended from cells to organs and to the body as a whole; we function best when our lives achieve a balance.

Self-care relates both to the necessary requirements to maintain a healthy body and mind – diet, exercise, sleep, rest, hygiene – and to one's psychological requirements – for social contact, pleasure, reward and psychological well-being. Between chores and pleasures, work and rest, and all the possible activities of self-care and daily living there is a substantial amount to balance!

Achieving a balance is particularly important for those who experience negative symptoms. If one is struggling to 'get by' it is common to neglect possible sources of pleasure and positive experiences as one focuses perceived limited resources on vital tasks. Extreme imbalance can lead to depression and to increased likelihood of relapse.

A checklist to help in exploring the client's lifestyle is presented in Box 2.6 and the key principles in Box 2.7. Weekly diary sheets, chores and pleasure monitoring and monthly activity logs can all be useful sources of information in examining lifestyle balance (Williams, 2004).

Box 2.6 Lifestyle balance checklist

- Exercise
- Diet
- Sleep pattern
- Chores
- Pleasures
- Mastery
- Social contact
- Personal care/hygiene/appearance
- Daily/weekly routine activities
- Treats and rewards
- Work
- Education

Box 2.7 Five key principles to maintaining a balanced lifestyle

1. *Optimise all basic requirements.* For example, although the body can survive on a poor or restricted diet, it is likely to function best when supplied with a range of nutrients, vitamins, minerals and a balance of the basic food groups. Similarly, while many people do habitually survive on limited sleep, we perform best on approximately 8 hours' sleep in a 24-hour period.
2. *Simplify.* Many activities are unavoidable and life can sometimes feel rushed and complex. Analysing one's use of time with the aim of minimising the effort involved often reveals areas where simplification is possible. For example, it might not be necessary to shop so often; shopping for perishable food once a week and for non-perishable food once a month can save time and effort. Similarly, sharing tasks with a friend or neighbour can reduce the energy expended on such tasks.
3. *Cultivate a positive attitude.* Chores are generally unavoidable; however, often the attitude we bring to tasks affects our experience of them. Finding ways of improving the experience of chores can make them less onerous and can even transform them into pleasures. For example, vacuuming could be viewed as an opportunity to 'work out' and be enhanced by listening to music or adding dance moves!
4. *Everything in moderation.* Balance can only be achieved if those areas which outweigh all others are checked and brought under control. The areas which require moderation vary from individual to individual but the most common is work. While it might not be possible to reduce the hours one works, ensuring regular breaks, taking regular annual leave, varying tasks undertaken and not taking work home are all strategies to reduce work becoming unbalanced. Doing too little can also become a habit which leads to imbalance: the less one does, the less one feels like doing. Imbalance can be identified by working out the hours spent in one's most common activities, eg watching television, sleeping, reading, and adjustments can be made if required.
5. *Cultivate self-compassion.* Looking after oneself, achieving and maintaining a balanced lifestyle can be viewed as acts of kindness and compassion towards oneself. Ultimately, if a person does not value themself, it is unlikely that they will strive to provide themself with a balanced and contented lifestyle.

Future planning can be helpful in maintaining focus, in fostering self-efficacy and in cultivating hope for the future. While the primary focus is on the present, having something to work towards is a primary motivator. Examining options and researching potential routes by which to attain them can be a very positive experience in itself and can help to set longer-term realistic goals. This might involve plans to start or return to work, to pursue education, training or to move house or location.

CLIENT INFORMATION SHEET 2.2 – UNDERSTANDING NEGATIVE SYMPTOMS

What are negative symptoms?

Negative symptoms are called 'negative' because they are seen as an absence of, or reduction in, the usual expected range of behaviours or experiences. They mainly affect emotions, motivation and behaviour. They can cause difficulties by interfering with work, education, relationships and social abilities; basically they affect quality of life.

Negative symptoms are a recognised group of problems which are commonly experienced by people with schizophrenia. Some people are more affected by these symptoms than they are by positive symptoms – such as hearing voices or having unusual beliefs. Other people are relatively unaffected or experience only mild symptoms from time to time and still others never experience these effects.

The five most common negative symptoms: the five As

Symptom name	Description	Experience
Avolition	Lack of energy, drive and interest in things.	Everything seems like a huge effort. Feeling drained of energy. Difficulty looking after oneself. Lack of curiosity about things.
Anhedonia	Loss of interest even in previously enjoyed activities. Inability to experience pleasure.	Not wanting to do things or go to places previously enjoyed. Giving up hobbies and interests.
Asociality	Lack of involvement in social relationships.	Not interested in other people. Difficulty keeping up relationships with family and friends. Not wanting to socialise.
Affective blunting	Reduced emotional expression, reactivity and feeling.	Showing less emotion. Feeling 'flat' and unemotional; smiling less, being less animated.
Alogia	Reduction in thinking and speech.	Difficulty holding conversations. Not knowing what to say or how to say it.

Related symptoms

Feelings of tiredness, loss of motivation, being 'slowed up' and having difficulties communicating with others are common in people who are depressed, anxious, have experienced a traumatic event or are experiencing significant stress. Such symptoms can also be caused by side effects of anti-psychotic medication. Your therapist will be able to discuss your symptoms with you to help you to learn more about them and what might be causing them.

Causes of negative symptoms

Negative symptoms are often misunderstood and seen as deliberate, as selfishness, laziness or stubbornness; they most definitely are not!

It is likely that there are biological reasons that so many people with schizophrenia experience the same type and range of difficulties. Some people are probably more susceptible to these types of problem because of their personality characteristics. There are also likely to be personal, social and psychological reasons why negative symptoms develop and continue to affect some people over quite long periods of time.

Negative symptoms can develop for many reasons:

- as a consequence of being in hospital for a long period of time
- as a way of reducing triggers to voices
- as a result of experiencing distressing beliefs
- as a way of coping with voices or distressing beliefs
- as a result of the trauma of mental illness
- as a defence against having too many demands
- as a response to being criticised
- due to pressure to live up to unrealistic expectations (from yourself or other people)
- demoralisation; not being able to perform as well as you used to
- as a response to reduced opportunities
- as a way of protecting yourself from fear of failure
- 'giving up' in response to loss caused by the illness, stigma or its consequences.

One or more of these reasons might apply to you, or other specific things might contribute to your experience of negative symptoms.

Great news!

Just as negative symptoms are caused and kept going in a variety of ways, so there are many methods of reducing their impact and of coping successfully with these difficulties.

Understanding your negative symptoms is the first big step towards overcoming them.

Psychological approaches to negative symptoms – focusing on your thoughts, feelings, behaviour and beliefs – have been found to be very helpful in tackling these symptoms.

CLIENT INFORMATION SHEET 2.3 – OVERCOMING NEGATIVE SYMPTOMS

As humans we are very good at coping with crises and acute problems; we automatically use 'survival' tactics to get us through them. Often our solutions work well in the short term, eg to avoid a threat or survive a shock, but over longer periods of time the solution itself can become the problem.

Doing less as a way of conserving energy works well when we are exhausted and need to rest. However, in the long term, the less we do, the less we feel like doing and our energy resources dwindle. Similarly, the more we avoid certain situations, the harder they seem to become.

Often, negative symptoms become entrenched habits which might have helped you to feel safe or to get through difficult experiences but have now become a pattern which is hard to break.

Three key points in combating negative symptoms:

1. A period of 'convalescence' is needed in the recovery from any serious illness. Sometimes 'less is more' – finding your own pace on the journey out of negative symptoms is important in restoring your mental strength.
2. Taking the pressure off enables us to feel better and, in time, to do more.
3. It is OK to aim lower and hit the target; over time the target can be raised and hit again.

CBT: Cognitive Behavioural Therapy

Research into psychological treatment of negative symptoms has shown that cognitive behavioural therapy can be very helpful in reducing these difficulties. People even continue to improve once the treatment has ended, and this suggests that the changes are long lasting because the person has learned to manage the symptoms themself. CBT works by looking at the way people think, feel and behave and understanding how these influence one's experiences. Often changing just one aspect can have a significant impact on the others.

CBT for negative symptoms focuses on four main areas:

1. The way that you *think*; for example about activities and interactions with other people. Identifying unhelpful thinking such as being too harsh on yourself or always imagining the worst possible outcome.
2. How you *feel* about yourself and your life. Exploring how thoughts can influence feelings and actions.
3. *Behaviour*; looking at interests and activities as well as your current ways of coping.
4. Examining underlying *beliefs* that might be affecting how you think, feel and behave.

Ways of overcoming negative symptoms

Together with your therapist you can develop an understanding of how your symptoms arose, what function they serve and what keeps them going (maintaining factors); this is called a formulation.

The formulation often produces ideas about how best to deal with your particular difficulties. There are many types of intervention, one or more (or all!) of these might be helpful to you:

- reducing demands
- looking at appraisals, beliefs and expectations, eg in relation to the likelihood of success, personal abilities and pleasurable experiences
- setting achievable short-term goals
- re-establishing daily routines/activity scheduling
- building resilience to stress
- problem solving
- setting achievable medium-term goals
- developing a balanced lifestyle
- planning for the future.

Remember that you are not alone. Many people have experienced negative symptoms and have learnt to overcome them.

A journey of a thousand miles begins with a single step.

Lau-Tzu, Chinese philosopher (604–531 BC)

3 Social **anxiety** disorder and **psychosis**

He who fears he shall suffer already suffers what he fears.

Montaigne

Social anxiety disorder, also known as social phobia, is characterised by intense fear in social situations. It causes considerable distress and impaired ability to function in at least some aspects of daily life. It can be either specific to certain situations such as speaking in public, or generalised across situations. Generalised social anxiety typically involves a persistent, intense, chronic fear of being judged by others and of being embarrassed or humiliated by one's own actions. The fear of social interaction is often accompanied by physical symptoms including palpations, nausea and stammering.

Lifetime prevalence rates in the general population are estimated to be approximately 13 per cent, making it the most common of the anxiety disorders.

Social anxiety disorder in people with psychosis

The presence of anxiety in clients with schizophrenia has been associated with a greater risk of suicide (Taiminen *et al*, 2001), poorer social functioning and an increased risk of relapse (Blanchard, 1998).

Social anxiety is very common in people with psychosis, affecting a significantly higher proportion than is affected in the general population.

Social anxiety can arise in the prodromal phase (Cunningham *et al*, 2005), during the acute phase and following symptomatic recovery. In the year following a first episode of psychosis a rate of 29 per cent has been reported (Birchwood *et al*, 2007). A study of out-patients with schizophrenia found 36.3 per cent had comorbid social anxiety disorder (Pallanti *et al*, 2004). The researchers suggest that social anxiety symptoms become most evident when clients are in remission from psychotic symptoms and reflect their greater efforts at social adaptation and increased expectations. Michail and Birchwood (2009) found social anxiety disorder effected 25 per cent of their sample of 80 people with first-episode psychosis, a further 16 per cent were diagnosed with an additional comorbid anxiety disorder, most common being panic disorder (10 per cent). It is of note that social anxiety problems were found to be distributed on a continuum from mild to moderate and severe; thus even those not meeting the criteria for a diagnosis of social anxiety disorder had some problems with social interaction.

Michail and Birchwood (2009) found that people with first-episode psychosis and social anxiety disorder reported comparable levels of social anxiety, autonomic symptoms, avoidance and depression as did those with social anxiety alone. Further, social anxiety in psychosis was found to be unrelated to positive symptoms including suspiciousness and persecution. A subgroup of socially anxious people with psychosis did express perceived threat from persecutors but this did not affect the severity of the anxiety; it appears that the majority of social anxiety disorder in psychosis is not qualitatively different from social anxiety in the general population.

The exact relationship between social anxiety and psychotic symptoms will, of course, vary among individuals and there is likely to be more than one causal pathway. Thus it is important to develop an individual formulation which considers possible links between the development and maintenance of social anxiety and of psychosis where they co-exist.

Michail and Birchwood (2009) propose three possible pathways to consider when exploring social anxiety in people with persecutory beliefs:

1. Social anxiety pre-dates the onset of the beliefs and serves to trigger and/or to maintain the persecutory beliefs.
2. Social anxiety and persecutory beliefs develop together and follow a similar course.
3. Social anxiety develops as a consequence of paranoid thinking.

A study of imagery experienced during social anxiety in clients with a diagnosis of psychosis found that some experienced social anxiety images typical of those with social anxiety alone whereas others experienced images that were more threatening and may be related to residual psychotic paranoia (Lockett *et al*, 2012). The researchers also found that image perspective varied in that typical social anxiety images tended to be seen from an observer perspective whereas those likely to be related to psychosis were more often seen from a field perspective. These findings have implications for treatment and suggest that while social anxiety based on fear of social judgement and expectations of being negatively appraised is likely to respond to CBT for social anxiety, social anxiety based on paranoid beliefs might best be addressed by CBT for paranoia (Lockett *et al*, 2012).

Assessment of social anxiety

There are three commonly used scales designed to measure social anxiety disorder.

The Social Interaction Anxiety Scale (SIAS) (Mattick and Clarke, 1998) contains 20 items rated on a five-point scale and measures anxiety in interpersonal situations. It assesses fears of general social interactions such as initiating and maintaining conversations with friends, strangers or potential partners. It corresponds to diagnostic descriptions of generalised social anxiety.

The Social Phobia Scale (SPS) (Mattick and Clarke, 1998) is the companion 20-item measure of specific fears of being scrutinised by others. It measures anxiety in situations such as public speaking, eating, drinking and writing. The scale corresponds to diagnostic descriptions of specific social anxiety.

Both scales have good internal consistency, test-retest reliability and are sensitive to treatment change.

The Fear of Negative Evaluation Scale (FNE) (Watson and Friend, 1969) assesses cognitions which are likely to maintain social phobia. It is a 30-item true/false scale designed to measure the degree to which people experience apprehension at the prospect of being evaluated negatively. There is also a 12-item version which correlates highly (.96) with the original scale (Leary, 1983).

Cognitive model of social phobia

A helpful and widely accepted model of social phobia is that advanced by Clark and Wells (1995) and Wells (1997). The model is presented in Figure 3.1. When a person enters a feared situation it activates assumptions about performance failure and showing anxiety symptoms. This perception of social danger leads to negative automatic thoughts. Such thoughts activate anxiety symptoms which, in turn, might be interpreted as evidence of failure and social humiliation. Appraisals of danger lead the person to become self-conscious – focusing on internal monitoring, self-observation and images of social humiliation. In an attempt to manage the situation, safety behaviours, such as avoiding eye contact, are employed; however, these serve to maintain the problem. If the feared situation is avoided this also maintains the problem as there is no opportunity to disconfirm negative appraisals. Anticipatory worry prior to a feared situation and post-event rumination both serve to maintain preoccupation with the feared situation.

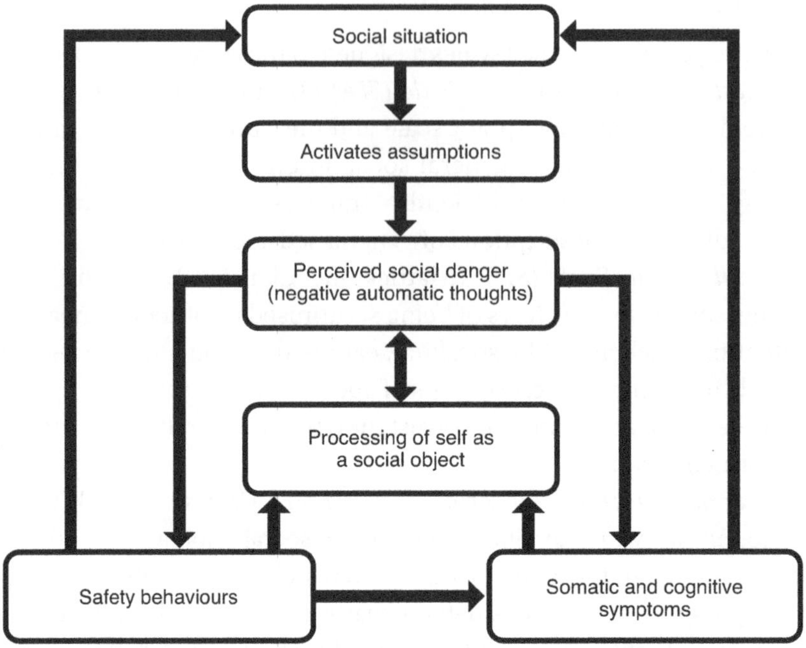

FIGURE 3.1 A cognitive model of social phobia

Reproduced with kind permission from Wells, Adrian (1997) *Social Phobia in Cognitive Therapy of Anxiety Disorders. A Practice Manual and Conceptual Guide*, Wiley, Chichester (Chapter Seven).

Guide to formulation in social anxiety disorder and psychosis

Developing a personalised understanding of the individual's social anxiety problems in the context of psychosis is vital as it is central to the development of appropriately targeted intervention. It also ensures that the social anxiety is specifically addressed rather than subsumed as 'part of the psychosis'. The guide presented in Box 3.1 summarises the main areas to address in developing a formulation of social anxiety disorder with your client.

Box 3.1 Guide to formulation of social anxiety disorder in people with psychosis

1. Identify any early social risk factors; these are often common to both the later development of social anxiety and of psychosis. They include: early traumatic experiences such as abuse, neglect and abandonment; deprivation; membership of marginalised social groups, such as immigrants; and impoverishment.

2. Establish any 'trait' dispositions, such as introversion or social avoidance which might have been present from early childhood. These, together with early social risk factors can be seen as 'vulnerability' factors for the development of social anxiety disorder.
3. Track the development of problems with interaction, social difficulties and social avoidance. Social anxiety tends to have its onset in childhood or early adolescence (Stein *et al*, 2001).
4. Assess for the presence and severity of other anxiety-related problems such as panic attacks, generalised anxiety and phobias, as well as depression. Try to establish the course of any such disorders; for example, did the social anxiety precede the depression or vice versa?
5. Elicit detailed descriptions of the specific cognitive, behavioural and autonomic symptoms of the social anxiety, as well as specific triggers. Automatic negative thoughts, beliefs and assumptions will form the basis of understanding the social anxiety in feared situations that can be explored in relation to the cognitive model.
6. Explore the course, severity and content of delusional beliefs in relation to the social anxiety. Persecutory threat, in particular, might play a role in the development and maintenance of the social anxiety. People with persecutory delusions often try to manage the perceived threat by avoiding 'high-risk' social encounters. Try to establish whether the social anxiety pre-dates the onset of persecutory beliefs, or whether it developed concurrently with persecutory thinking or as a consequence of paranoid ideation.
7. Examine other positive psychotic symptoms – such as auditory hallucinations – in relation to the social anxiety. Social fears and disengagement might be anticipated in those who hear voices that are derogatory or that directly undermine trust in others. Explore imagery experienced during social anxiety; what is its content, nature and perspective? Try to determine the causal pathway.
8. Assess the impact of the social anxiety on all aspects of the person's life: education, employment, social contacts, activities of daily living. Also address the possible relative contribution of social anxiety to adverse events such as hospitalisation, suicide attempts.
9. Consider the role of shame, perceived social 'subordination' and stigma that the person might experience as a result of their diagnosis and 'patient status'.
10. Establish the role of 'safety behaviours' in maintaining the social anxiety. People who fear they will humiliate themselves in public or be 'found out' are likely to compound their social phobia by avoidance.

SOCIAL ANXIETY CASE EXAMPLE: MARK

Mark is a 21-year-old man who has lived with his grandmother since the death of his mother two years ago. He has no recollection of his father who left when Mark was a baby; he has no siblings. At age 10, Mark developed school phobia and was home taught by his mother for the last year of his junior education. He returned to secondary school where he did not fit in and was intimidated, rejected and ignored by his peers. He did not attend any social events, did not invite other children home and isolated himself when his mother had visitors. He passed his exams at age 16 years and moved to a college to study 'A' levels. However, he started to feel 'disconnected', did not make any friends and on several occasions felt humiliated when he was unable to speak in front of the class. He experienced an acute psychotic episode in which he believed that he was being persecuted for being an apostle. He was hospitalised for four months. Mark made a good recovery and returned to college part time. He successfully completed his 'A' levels but was unable to find work on leaving college; this was mainly due to being unable to perform at interview. When his mother died, he refused to leave the house for several months. He was prescribed anti-depressants and was eventually persuaded to move in with his maternal grandmother. He recently decided to return to education and applied to study computing at a local college. However, after attending the open evening he withdrew his application and again refused to leave the house. His general practitioner referred him to a clinical psychologist.

Formulation for Mark

Mark was able to identify that his feeling of being 'different' from others arose when he was in primary school. He had always been a shy boy; he had been very close to his mother and only felt relaxed when in her company; he thought that this led to his school phobia at age 10. Never having known his father and the sense of abandonment that he felt were likely to have been contributory social risk factors. Although being home taught was helpful at the time it added to his worries about talking to others and he had greater difficulty 'fitting in' on his return to school. The exclusion he experienced from his peers furthered his negative assumptions about himself and reinforced his coping strategy of avoidance of social contact when possible. Mark described acute anxiety and panic attacks during his initial weeks at college; he experienced depersonalisation and derealisation. This led to his acute psychotic episode in which he believed that the explanation for his difference and perceived persecution was due to his being Mark the apostle.

Following his recovery he began to feel ashamed of the beliefs he had voiced and feared others knowing that he had been diagnosed with schizophrenia.

This contributed to increased awkwardness with people; he avoided eye contact, experienced chest pains and began to stutter if required to talk. The death of his mother was devastating for Mark: he had lost the only person with whom he felt comfortable and he was unable to leave the house as the anticipation of people giving their condolences was unbearable. The medication was likely to have had some anxiolytic effect and he was able to think about his future. He described anticipatory anxiety at having to attend the open evening and his fears were realised when a student asked him a question; he later ruminated on his socially inadequate performance and perceived humiliation which led him to decide that he could not attend college.

Mark's social anxiety pre-dates the onset of psychosis and social fears are likely to have contributed to the psychotic episode. The experience of the delusional belief and subsequent hospitalisation contributed to increasing self-consciousness and negative self-image.

Mark examined the current situation with his therapist using the cognitive model as shown in Figure 3.2.

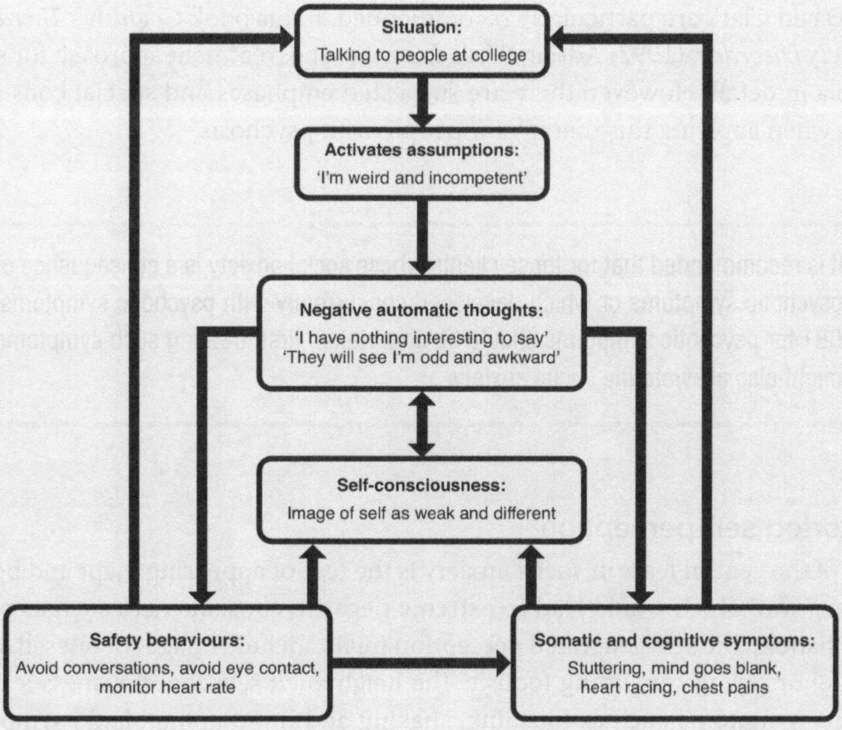

FIGURE 3.2 Cognitive model for Mark's social anxiety

Treatment of social anxiety

CBT for social anxiety has been found to be effective. A meta-analytic review concluded that treatments involving multiple components which include cognitive and behavioural interventions are particularly effective (Taylor, 1996). Such CBT typically includes developing a cognitive-behavioural understanding of symptoms, cognitive restructuring and exposure to anxiety-producing situations.

There is evidence that such interventions are also effective in social anxiety and psychosis. A CBT group-based intervention of eight sessions was found to be successful in treating social anxiety in people with schizophrenia; the intervention group improved on measures including the Brief Social Phobia Scale and Social Interaction Anxiety Scale, whereas a control group showed no change in symptomatology (Halperin *et al*, 2000).

As social anxiety in people with psychosis has been found to be indistinguishable from that in social phobia alone (Michail and Birchwood, 2009), the well-established treatment interventions known to work well with social anxiety are also recommended for people with psychosis whose anxiety is based upon fear of social judgement and negative evaluation. The CBT approach of Adrian Wells and David Clark are particularly recommended. In his book *Cognitive Therapy of Anxiety Disorders* (1997) Adrian Wells describes the treatment approach for social phobia in detail. However, there are suggested emphases and special considerations when applying this therapy for people with psychosis.

> It is recommended that for those clients whose social anxiety is a consequence of psychotic symptoms or which developed concurrently with psychotic symptoms, CBT for psychotic symptoms should be undertaken first: treating such symptoms might also alleviate the social anxiety.

Distorted self-perception

One of the central fears in social anxiety is the fear of appearing inept and behaving in a way which would lead to extreme negative consequences such as public humiliation. The self-generated perception might include images of oneself losing control or saying something foolish. The heightened self-consciousness leads to anxiety symptoms such as blushing, shaking and mind going blank, symptoms that, in turn, lead to greater fear that humiliation is imminent. In people with psychosis this self-consciousness is all the more likely if they have previously behaved in a bizarre or unusual manner or have experienced loss of control over some aspect of their behaviour. Thus the fear is not merely of anticipated possible disaster but is often based on previous experience. As there is often truth in the possibility that the feared event might occur, eg one's speech might indeed be inhibited by hearing voices or one's mind could 'go blank' by thought blocking, this needs to be addressed collaboratively in therapy. *See* Box 3.2 for treatment for distorted self-perception.

Box 3.2 Addressing distorted self-perception

Does tangible evidence exist?
If no: examine self-appraisal via guided discovery.
If yes: examine the evidence, how strong is the evidence?

- If appropriate, dispute the validity of the evidence. For example, the person might have previously experienced thought blocking but this symptom has remitted and is no longer problematic.
- If appropriate, positively reframe the experience in more realistic terms. This can be done by generating alternative explanations for the evidence or by examining any thinking errors in the interpretation. For example, the difficulty in talking to others while in hospital was likely to have been due to sedative effects of medication and the interference of florid symptoms rather than social incompetence.
- If the evidence is strong, look at ways of overcoming this. For example, if derogatory voices are causing social distress, tackle these with CBT for auditory hallucinations.

Distorted 'other' perception

People with social anxiety tend to focus on a negative, self-generated perception of their social performance and assume that this is also the way in which others view them. They are often sensitive to negative evaluations by others and over-emphasise the extent to which they are observed and scrutinised by others, eg they might think that everyone notices them when they enter a room and judges them negatively.

Although it is gradually becoming more acceptable to have a mental illness, people with psychosis are indeed 'judged' and stigmatised.

In addition, some people might have experienced times of intense scrutiny by others, either when in hospital or when 'monitored' by mental health professionals or carers in the community. In hospital it is not uncommon for observations of the patient's behaviour and interactions to be written in the medical notes every few hours. Often discharge from hospital can be conditional on 'appropriate' social behaviour. *See* Box 3.3 for treatment for distorted 'other' perception. Acknowledge and discuss the experiences of stigma that the client has personally experienced and relate this to the possible effect on social anxiety.

Box 3.3 Addressing distorted 'other' perception

- Examine the likelihood of beliefs such as 'they will know I have a mental illness' (how would they know?) or 'they are prejudiced against me because I haven't got a job' (if they are, is their view important?)
- Explore the likely contribution of real experiences of scrutiny, by mental health professionals, carers and others on the client's social anxiety.
- Are there any current pressures on social performance? If so, examine the validity of these.
- The meaning and implication of fears of social judgement should be explored. Often these meanings are amenable to modification in cognitive therapy. For example, 'If people stare at me it's because I am no good.'
- Challenge the assumed consequences of poor social performance. (What would really happen? Does that happen to other people? Is that so bad?)

Thinking errors

We probably would not worry about what people think of us if we could know how seldom they do.

Olin Miller

Interestingly, the three most common thinking errors in social anxiety are also typical of cognitive distortions in psychosis: mind reading, predicting the future and personalising.

Mind reading is the assumption that people are reacting negatively to one when there is no supporting evidence, eg 'she thinks I am stupid'.

Predicting the future involves dwelling on the worst possible outcome and overestimating the probability that it will occur, eg 'I know that I will stutter and blush and everyone will laugh at me'.

Personalising is relating external events to oneself when there is no obvious basis for this, eg 'everyone is arguing because I am here'.

Recognising and challenging such thinking errors helps to invalidate negative automatic thoughts and beliefs. A common method is the 'triple column technique' (Burns, 1989) in which the client writes down their thoughts and rational alternatives; *see* Box 3.4.

Box 3.4 Triple column technique

- Column 1: Write down automatic negative thoughts as they occur and rate belief in thought on a scale of 0–100.
- Column 2: Identify and label thinking errors, eg personalising.
- Column 3: Substitute a rational response for each thought and rate belief in alternative response on a scale of 0–100.

These records can be reviewed in session in order to monitor and reinforce progress.

Rational-response 'flash cards' can also be constructed and carried to help to remind the person of an alternative self-statement and the supporting evidence. For example, 'I worry that she thinks I'm stupid but this is just "mind reading". Evidence: she asks my opinion, she is friendly, she smiles at me.'

Anxiety symptoms

Symptoms of anxiety include cognitive symptoms, such as racing thoughts or one's mind going blank, and physiological symptoms: blushing, shaking, sweating, stuttering, babbling, shaky voice, crying, trembling, feeling hot, feeling paralysed and breathlessness. Such symptoms are elicited by negative automatic thoughts and increase self-consciousness thereby escalating the anxiety with thoughts such as 'they can see me blushing, I must look ridiculous'. People with experience of psychosis involving racing thoughts or one's mind going blank might also fear the onset of a psychotic episode, or memories of such might be triggered. Treatment suggestions are presented in Box 3.5.

Box 3.5 Addressing anxiety symptoms

- Provide information and education about anxiety symptoms and their generation in social situations; in particular that such symptoms are the result of negative assumptions and cognitions – they are not indicators of psychosis.
- Worries regarding conspicuousness of symptoms can be reduced by recording the client (audio or audio-visual, as appropriate) in a situation known to produce anxiety symptoms. The actual presentation is then contrasted with the self-generated image to reveal that in reality such symptoms are generally inconspicuous.
- Encourage the client to substitute the more accurate image in future social situations.
- Rational self-statements can also be generated from the realistic self-image, eg 'my symptoms are hardly noticeable'.

Safety behaviours

Fear makes strangers of people who would be friends.

Shirley MacLaine

Safety behaviours such as mental rehearsal of what to say or avoidance of eye contact are used in a bid to avert the feared event; however, unfortunately they frequently maintain or even aggravate the problem. This happens in three ways.

- Exacerbating symptoms, eg enhanced vigilance of internal states such as monitoring heart rate or breathing, can lead to increased preoccupation, self-consciousness and hyper-arousal.
- Secondly, some safety behaviours affect the person's presentation to others making them appear aloof, distant and unfriendly – eg avoiding eye contact, giving only brief responses – this reduces the chances of successful social interaction.
- Thirdly, successful social interactions are likely to be attributed to the use of the safety behaviour, and therefore do not weaken (and sometimes strengthen) negative assumptions and distorted cognitions. People with psychosis, especially

Box 3.6 Addressing safety behaviours

- Demonstrate the effects of safety behaviours by encouraging the client to engage in a feared social encounter (either with the therapist in session or in vivo) with all safety behaviours employed to the full and again while abandoning all safety behaviours. The effect on 1) physical symptoms, 2) social performance, and 3) self-consciousness can then be gauged by contrasting the two experiences. Clients invariably find that dropping safety behaviours reduces physical symptoms, increases their social performance and reduces self-consciousness.
- Similarly, the paradoxical technique of inviting the client to increase self-focus, eg by concentrating on their anxiety symptoms and how bad they feel in a social situation also illustrates that self-focus and symptoms are closely related. Repeating the exercise while the client is instructed to focus on aspects of the external environment reinforces the concept that self-focus is a hindrance, not a help.
- Reducing avoidance of social situations is central to enabling the person to reattribute negative thoughts and to challenge assumptions. Gradual exposure to feared situations (while abandoning safety behaviours) and processing and discussing the disconfirmatory evidence so gathered are vital to reducing social anxiety.

those who experience persecutory beliefs, paranoid ideation and derogatory voices, often use avoidance and hyper-vigilance as coping strategies. Isolating oneself and focusing on potential threats, both internal and external, are likely to exacerbate social anxiety by heightening self-focus and preventing disconfirmation.

Behavioural interventions which focus on the elimination of safety behaviours are particularly helpful in treating social anxiety. *See* Box 3.6.

CLIENT INFORMATION SHEET 3.1 – SOCIAL ANXIETY

Social anxiety is one of the most common of the anxiety disorders. It affects about 13 per cent of the population. In people with psychosis it is even more common; approximately one-third of people might be affected at some point in their life.

What is social anxiety?

Social anxiety disorder, sometimes known as social phobia, is a fear of situations which might lead to embarrassment. In these situations the person experiences unpleasant anxiety symptoms and the fear interferes with the person's life. Sometimes being in the situation, or just thinking about it leads to panic attacks. The fear that other people will judge the person as weak, foolish or stupid is common in social anxiety. Feared situations can be specific – eg speaking or eating in public – or might include many social situations including conversations with family, friends and others and being in public places.

Common symptoms in social anxiety

Anxiety symptoms such as heart palpitations and rapid breathing are common to all anxiety disorders. However, the symptoms most troubling in social anxiety are those which one fears that others will notice: blushing, stammering, sweating, shaking and becoming 'tongue-tied'.

What causes social anxiety?

Social anxiety often develops in childhood and some things might make a person more likely to develop it: being a naturally shy person, having trouble fitting in or having traumatic experiences such as losing a parent or being abused or neglected. These factors can also make a person more vulnerable to developing psychosis which is perhaps why social anxiety is so common in people with psychosis.

Social anxiety might develop before psychosis or as a result of having psychosis. Experiences such as hearing critical voices or believing that people are threatening or dangerous might, understandably, cause some people to fear social situations. Feeling stigmatised, discriminated against or embarrassed due to the diagnosis might also contribute to social anxiety.

Understanding social anxiety

Here is a typical sequence of events:

1. You enter a social situation, eg eating in a café.
2. This causes underlying beliefs to be triggered, eg 'I will do something to make me look stupid', 'I will be humiliated'.
3. This creates negative automatic thoughts, eg 'I will shake and blush, everyone will look at me, I could drop my tray'.
4. The thoughts create anxiety symptoms, eg trembling and blushing.
5. The anxiety symptoms cause increased self-focus and self-consciousness which can lead to more negative thoughts, eg 'I am shaking, everyone can see how anxious I am', 'I look foolish'.
6. In an attempt to cope with the situation, 'safety behaviour' such as avoiding eye contact or rushing are used. These often make the situation worse and draw more attention from others causing more self-consciousness.
7. After the event, the worst aspects of the situation are remembered and gone over in one's mind. This is likely to add to future beliefs, eg 'I can't cope with eating in public', and the creation of more safety behaviours, eg 'I will avoid eating with others whenever I can'.

Treatment of social anxiety

Fortunately there is a very successful treatment for social anxiety called Cognitive Behavioural Therapy (CBT). This involves understanding how the social anxiety developed, what triggers it and what keeps it going.

There are a number of methods and techniques which can reduce social anxiety and its symptoms. These include:

- looking at underlying beliefs and the meaning of the beliefs
- tackling negative automatic thoughts and thinking errors
- reducing self-focus
- dropping safety behaviours
- improving self-image accuracy
- challenging worries before, during and after the situation
- reducing avoidance.

Nobody can make you feel inferior without your consent.

Eleanor Roosevelt

4 Obsessional compulsive disorder and psychosis

Obsessional compulsive disorder (OCD) is an anxiety disorder in which the person experiences recurrent obsessions and/or compulsions that are time consuming and/or cause significant distress or impairment. Obsessions are persistent intrusive and/or inappropriate thoughts, impulses or images. Compulsions are repetitive behaviours which can be overt or covert. Table 4.1 lists the range of obsessions and compulsions typically found in OCD. Lifetime prevalence of OCD in the general population is estimated to be 2.5 per cent.

TABLE 4.1 Types of obsessions and compulsions

Type	Examples
Obsessions:	
Contamination	Germs, poisons, infestation
Doubting	Door left unlocked, electrical items left on, accidentally injured someone
Aggressive	Urge to harm children, punch someone, run down with car
Sexual	Imagery of pornographic or unacceptable acts
Somatic	Worry over potentially serious or unusual medical symptoms
Blasphemous	Shouting out in church
Overt compulsions	Hand washing, checking, ordering, cleaning, alignment of objects
Covert compulsions	Praying, counting, repeating words

Note that most obsessions have 'moral' themes which are more likely to assume personal significance.

It has been suggested that the most common obsessions found in clients with OCD and psychosis are contamination, aggression and somatic obsessions and that the most typical compulsions are cleaning or washing, checking, repeating and counting (Kruger *et al*, 2000).

Prevalence and prognostic significance of OCD in psychosis

The co-existence of obsessional compulsive symptoms in people diagnosed with schizophrenia was described over 100 years ago (Bleuler, 1911). The association was also documented by Schneider in his writings on compulsive states in schizophrenia in 1925. Although a large body of knowledge now exists on both OCD and psychosis, surprisingly little is known about the links between the disorders. It has been suggested that the limited literature on OCD and schizophrenia indicates that their co-occurrence is under-identified (Kruger *et al*, 2000).

This is particularly pertinent because, when specifically assessed, the prevalence of OC symptoms in people with a diagnosis of schizophrenia is high. One study found that 25 per cent of 102 patients with chronic schizophrenia had significant OC symptoms. In addition the group with OCD had earlier-onset psychosis, spent more time in hospital and had lower social and employment functioning (Berman *et al*, 1995). Based on the prevalence rates of schizophrenia and OCD in the community, the expected co-occurrence rate is 2 per cent (Foa and Kozak, 1995). A typical prevalence rate of 15.8 per cent found in a sample of 76 people with schizophrenia is therefore seven times higher than chance (Kruger *et al*, 2000).

Fenton and McGlashan (1986) looked at the clinical characteristics and long-term course of 21 people with schizophrenia and prominent OC symptoms. The two groups were not distinguishable on admission; however, the group with OC and schizophrenia had significantly worse long-term outcome and was almost uniformly poorer on a range of measures including social relations, employment, psychopathology and global functioning. Fenton and McGlashan (1986) conclude that persistent OC symptoms are a powerful predictor of poor prognosis in schizophrenia. It is not clear whether this is because the OCD remains untreated, because OCD hampers the treatment of psychosis or because the co-morbid condition exacerbates psychosis.

Links between OCD and psychosis

As with other disorders that are co-morbid with psychosis, there are three possible pathways which link OCD and psychosis.

1. The OCD pre-dates the psychosis and serves to trigger psychotic symptoms. It has been postulated that childhood OCD might be a precursor of adult psychosis (Rosenburg, 1967). In a sample of people with schizophrenia and OCD, many were found to have developed OCD in childhood prior to the onset of schizophrenia (Kruger *et al*, 2000).
2. The OCD and psychosis develop together and follow a similar course. There is evidence of the involvement of the frontal lobe and the basal ganglia in the pathophysiology of both schizophrenia and OCD (Gray, 1994).

3. OCD develops as a consequence of psychotic symptoms. For example, experience of persecutory delusions might lead to increased vigilance and efforts to control the environment, thus generating obsessional ruminations and checking compulsions.

In their small study of 15 patients with OCD and psychosis, Ganesan and colleagues (2001) found that OCD pre-dated the onset of psychosis in a third of cases, whereas both disorders developed simultaneously in 40 per cent and psychosis developed prior to OCD in just under a third (27 per cent). It is possible that schizophrenia with OCD represents not true co-morbidity, but a subtype of schizophrenia. Further, due to the similarities and overlap between the two disorders, it is possible that in some cases schizophrenia represents the severe end of an OCD continuum. Indeed, occasionally severe OCD might be misdiagnosed as psychosis (Hwang and Opler, 1994).

Kruger and her colleagues (2000) point out that many OCD symptoms involving motion, thought and perception can be placed on continuums which, at the severe end, merge with schizophrenia, eg from mild tics to catatonia; from circumstantial movements to stereotyped mannerisms; from obsessional thoughts to delusions. Consideration of where the person's symptoms lie on these continuums can assist in formulation, assessment and treatment (*see* Box 4.1).

It is also the case that people with psychosis share particular characteristics with those with OCD. For example, both tend to hold superstitious beliefs, engage in magical thinking and show characteristic 'thought-action' fusion – such as 'if I think a bad thought it is more likely that it could happen'. Both also tend to predict negative outcomes and such thinking can lead to making catastrophic misinterpretations. Aberrant salience, the tendency to ascribe personal meaning and significance to events, is another commonality.

Interestingly, findings indicate that the co-existence of OCD does not have a significant impact on the psychotic symptomatology and that people with both diagnoses cannot be distinguished from those with schizophrenia alone on a measure of positive and negative symptoms (Berman *et al*, 1998). However, one study found higher rates of negative symptoms in people with schizophrenia and OCD (Fenton and McGlashen, 1986). Others found less suspiciousness in people with both disorders (Kruger *et al*, 2000).

Assessment of OCD

Three commonly used inventories for the assessment of OCD symptomatology are:

- *Maudsley Obsessive-Compulsive Inventory (MOCI)* (Hodgson and Rachman, 1977). The MOCI is a 30-item true/false self-report questionnaire. It produces a total score consisting of four subscale scores: checking, cleaning, slowness and doubting. The emphasis is on behavioural rather than cognitive symptoms.

- *Obsessive-Compulsive Inventory (OCI)* (Foa *et al*, 1998). This 42-item inventory measures frequency and distress. There are seven subscales: washing, checking, doubting, ordering, obsessions, hoarding and neutralising.
- *Padua Inventory (PI)* (Sanavio, 1988). This is a 60-item rating scale in which degree of disturbance is rated on a five-point scale. There are four factors: impaired control over mental events, contamination fears, checking behaviours and urges and worries about losing control over motor behaviour.

Specific measures which access the clients' thoughts, beliefs and cognitive biases are particularly useful when conducting CBT:

- *Metacognitions Questionnaire (MCQ)* (Cartwright-Hatton and Wells, 1997). This 65-item questionnaire uses a four-point rating scale. Five factors are measured: 1) positive beliefs about worry; 2) negative beliefs about the uncontrollability of thoughts and their danger; 3) loss of cognitive confidence; 4) superstition and responsibility beliefs in relation to one's thoughts; 5) 'cognitive self-consciousness' – the tendency to be aware of one's thoughts.
- *Thought-Action Fusion Scale-Revised (TAF-S)* (Shafran *et al*, 1996). Clients respond on a five-point scale to 19 items divided into three scales. The TAF-moral scale assesses the belief that thinking about something is as morally unacceptable as acting on it. The TAF-likelihood for others scale assesses the belief that thinking about a negative event happening to others increases the chances of it happening. The TAF-likelihood for self scale assesses this in relation to the event happening to one's self.
- *Magical Ideation Scale (MIS)* (Eckblad and Chapman, 1983). This 30-item true/false scale measures belief in a number of 'magical' influences, eg thought transmission, spirit influences, astrology, good luck charms, psychic energy. Some items assess ideas of reference which might be regarded as psychotic symptoms. The scale was originally designed as an indicator of proneness to psychosis.
- *Illusory Beliefs Inventory (IBI)* (Kingdon *et al*, 2012) is a 24-item measure of magical thinking. It has three subscales representing domains of magical beliefs, spirituality and internal state and thought-action fusion.
- *Responsibility Attitudes Scale (RAS)* (Salkovskis *et al*, 2000) is a general belief measure linked to responsibility assumptions commonly found in people with OCD. It is scored on a seven-point scale.

Working model of OCD

Wells (1997) has produced a succinct working model of OCD which assists formulation and helps clients to conceptualise the problem. The model shows the relationship between beliefs, behaviour and emotion in OCD. The model is presented in Figure 4.1.

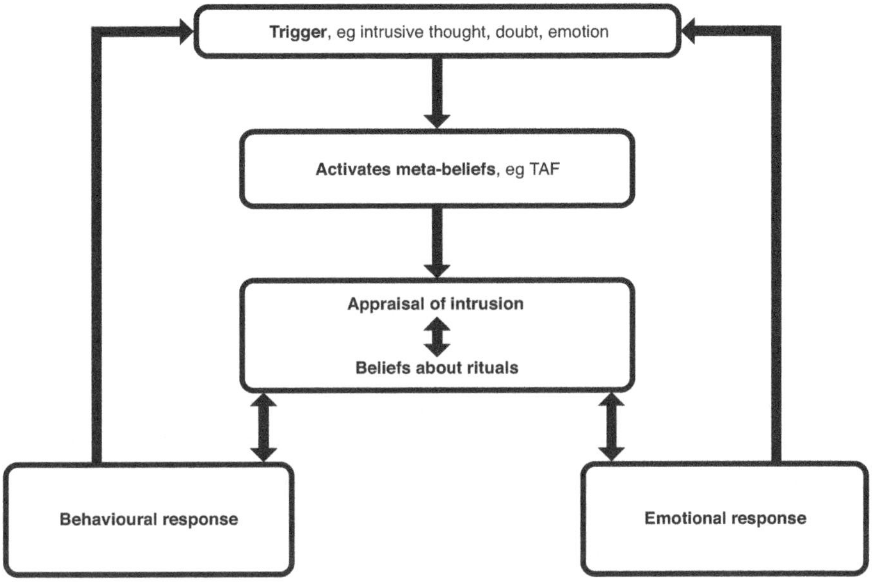

FIGURE 4.1 Cognitive model of obsessional compulsive disorder

Reproduced with kind permission from Wells, Adrian (1997) *Social Phobia in Cognitive Therapy of Anxiety Disorders. A Practice Manual and Conceptual Guide*, Wiley, Chichester (Chapter Nine).

A trigger, eg a thought of harming one's child, activates beliefs about the meaning of the trigger, eg 'thinking this thought makes it likely that I could do it'.

These beliefs influence the appraisal of the intrusions, eg 'this is a dangerous thought, I am a dangerous person'.

In addition, the person's beliefs about rituals and behavioural responses further influence and reinforce the appraisals, eg 'If I don't suppress this thought I will act it out. If I repeat "don't do it" then I won't do it'.

Negative emotional reactions are produced in response to the beliefs and appraisals and can lead to further negative appraisals, eg fear and anxiety can produce symptoms such as palpitations and might be interpreted as 'I am losing control' which in turn increases the potency of the original trigger: 'I could hurt my child'.

Similarly, the behavioural responses can also serve to maintain the problem such as when attempted suppression of thoughts produces a paradoxical increase in thoughts. In the same way, attempts to neutralise intrusions, eg by hand washing, can maintain preoccupation. Engaging in rituals such as checking, repeating or counting can also increase the range of associations between stimuli and intrusions.

The role of neutralisation is typically to prevent the feared event occurring, thus disconfirmation is prevented and the belief is strengthened, eg 'if I had not cancelled out the impulse to hurt my child I would have hurt him'. This cycle is frequently repeated and strengthened:

Obsession → neutralisation → relief → confirmation of belief

(Rachman, 2003)

Ten-point guide to formulation of OCD in clients with psychosis

The working model helps to direct formulation. However, there are several special considerations with clients who have OCD in addition to psychosis. The following guidance summarises the main areas to be explored in development of the formulation.

1. Collate and detail each OC symptom, including origin, history, frequency, duration, preoccupation and distress.
2. Try to track the association between the OC symptoms and psychotic symptoms, eg which started first? What are the similarities and differences between the symptoms?
3. It can be helpful to assess symptoms on continuums. It is likely that severe OCD merges with psychotic symptoms at the extreme ends of the continuums. There are also potential symptom overlaps, eg over-valued ideas and magical thinking and these can help to understand the links between OC and psychotic symptoms. Continuums are shown in Box 4.1
4. Explore external triggers such as situations which evoke intrusions, eg walking away from home might instigate a checking compulsion. Look at exposure to specific cues pertinent to the belief, eg knives for someone with an obsessional fear of harming.
5. Explore internal triggers, eg low mood, anger, irritability, stress, voices.
6. Investigate cognitive responses to the trigger; these are often characteristic biases and beliefs such as thought-action fusion, thought-event fusion, inflated responsibility and perfectionistic ideation.
7. Examine the perceived meaning and significance of the beliefs, ie negative appraisals about intrusions. People with psychosis and those with OCD are prone to find personal significance in thoughts; this increased salience is

Box 4.1 Obsessive compulsive – psychotic symptoms continuums

Perceptual symptoms

Intrusive images ______ Visual hallucinations

Cognitive symptoms

Obsessional thoughts ______ Thought disorder

Intrusive thoughts ______ Delusional belief

(Overvalued ideas and magical thinking as intermediate)

Impulses

Suppressed impulses ______ Irresistable urge

(Acted out)

Motor symptoms

Minor tics ______ Catatonia

Insight

Full recognition ______ No recognition

(Excessive/unreasonable)

another common factor between the two disorders. Personal meanings might include: 'these thoughts show that I am a dangerous person', 'these thoughts show that I could die', 'these thoughts show that I am evil', 'these thoughts show that I could kill'. Appraisals might also include fears of becoming mentally ill or suffering a relapse.

8. Investigate behavioural responses and beliefs about the responses. Responses might include rumination, overt and covert 'neutralising' of the intrusion such as by counting, checking, or alignment of objects or other rituals designed to counteract the intrusion. Beliefs about the behaviour can include positive benefits, eg 'counting prevents me from acting on the thought', as well as negative beliefs, eg 'constant rumination will make me ill'. Ask about the perceived consequences of relinquishment, eg fear of loss of control. Also assess any rituals or compulsions in relation to all coping strategies for psychotic symptoms, eg use of talisman to ward off voices.
9. Explore the role of emotional responses. These are likely to include negative emotional states such as fear, anger, anxiety, guilt and shame. As with the behavioural responses, examine beliefs about the emotions, eg how are they appraised? Do they maintain the intrusions? Appraisals might include 'I am

scared therefore something bad is about to happen', or 'my heart is racing therefore I am losing control'.

10. Assess perceived control over responses and any associated psychotic beliefs, eg of being controlled or manipulated.

CASE VIGNETTE: MONICA

Monica is a 23-year-old woman who lives alone. As a child she was very conscientious and reported being fastidious about her appearance. Her mother raised Monica and her younger brother alone following the suicide of her father when Monica was three. Her mother had generalised anxiety disorder and suffered panic attacks. Monica reported that as her mother was often scared to leave the house, she would therefore buy food on the way home from school and would prepare family meals from the age of 11. Monica reported experiencing obsessional thoughts from age 10 including worries that her mother would die and images of her mother dying of a heart attack. She worried that she needed to be 'the perfect daughter' or she would be punished by her fears coming true. At age 21 Monica left home and moved into a flat near to her mother and brother so that she could continue to look after them. Within a year she experienced an acute psychotic episode in which she believed that she could control other people's actions and could read their thoughts. Monica was admitted to an acute psychiatric ward where she experienced auditory hallucinations. She was discharged after one month with community follow-up. Although she improved on medication, Monica continued to experience residual psychotic symptoms: benign voices which gave her instructions, eg 'finish your tea', 'sit down', 'walk more slowly'. Although she was not troubled by these symptoms, she started to think that her voices were contagious and feared that other people – specifically her mother and brother – would also hear voices and be admitted to psychiatric hospital. She developed a number of neutralising behaviours including hand washing and showering to prevent possible contagion.

Formulation for Monica

With the help of her therapist, Monica was able to identify that her belief that her voices were contagious originated from her interpretation that she herself 'caught' the voices in psychiatric hospital. She had not experienced auditory hallucinations prior to hospitalisation and concluded that being with patients who heard voices had led her to develop the same symptoms.

Misinterpretation of the language of 'illness' in which she was immersed during her stay in hospital reinforced this belief, eg she was told 'stay away from him, he is very unwell', and 'the medication and rest will build up your resistance'.

Monica's catastrophic appraisal that she could pass on her illness to her mother and brother appeared to have been driven both by her inflated sense of responsibility – 'I am responsible for my mother's health' – as well as feelings of guilt at having 'abandoned them'.

Monica's attempts to neutralise the effects of the voices led to compulsive hand washing and showering after which she felt relief that she had 'averted disaster', hence reinforcing the erroneous belief. Anxiety symptoms such as sweating and palpitations also reinforced her notion of 'being ill' and hence, contagious.

Monica was tense and worried on her daily visits to her mother due to the fear of passing on the voices. This heightened level of stress and anxiety seemed to increase the likelihood of experiencing voices hence setting up a vicious cycle which exacerbated symptoms.

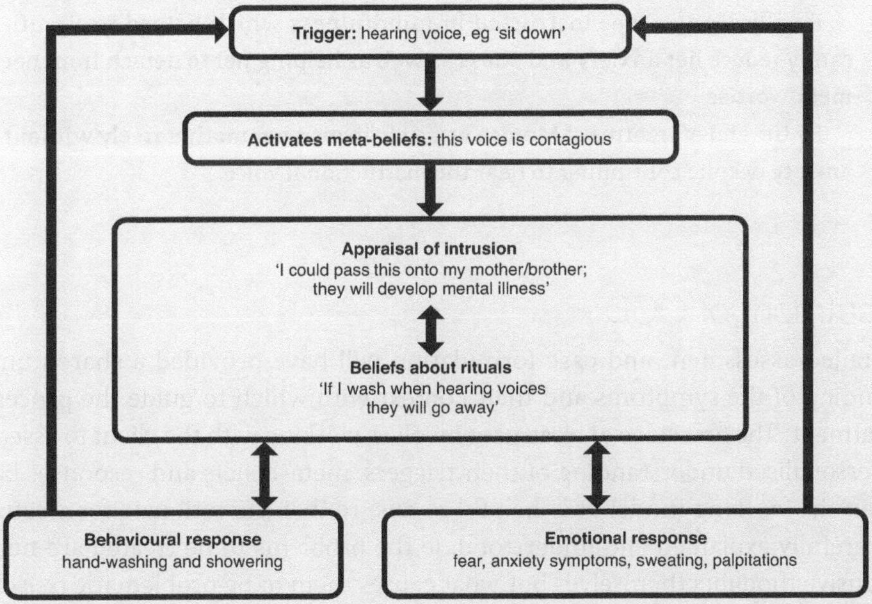

FIGURE 4.2 Formulation for Monica

Treatment for Monica

Monica was introduced to the working model of OCD and was able to develop a personalised model of her own symptoms. She was provided with information and education about the course of psychosis including identification of the prodromal phase and development of acute symptoms followed by remission. This helped her to understand that the timing of the development of auditory hallucinations was in line with the usual pattern and was not dependent on being with people with psychosis.

The formulation indicated that treatment focused on behavioural experiments to see whether voices are contagious might be beneficial. Monica was invited to conduct a mini-survey of 10 mental health workers to ask about their personal experience of hearing voices. Contrary to her prediction, she found that, despite a combined total of 135 years of working with clients who hear voices, none of the people surveyed had personally experienced hearing a voice.

Results of this experiment gave Monica courage to attempt a more threatening behavioural experiment – trying to make the therapist 'catch' the voices by standing near the therapist when hearing the voice without neutralising.

Following on from the successful completion of this procedure, Monica was eventually able to conduct a similar exposure and response-prevention experiment with her brother as the 'target'.

Finally Monica was instructed in mindfulness which helped to significantly reduce her anxiety and stress as well as helping her to detach from her meta-worries.

By the end of treatment Monica was able to visit her mother freely without anxiety despite continuing to hear the instructional voice.

Treatment of OCD

Detailed assessment and case formulation will have provided a shared understanding of the symptoms and their context with which to guide the process of treatment. The first stage of treatment involves working with the client to assemble a personalised understanding of their triggers, meta-beliefs and responses based upon the working model. It is helpful to ensure that the rationale for treatment is carefully explained and understood, ie the problems to be treated are not the intrusive thoughts themselves but what causes them to be problematic (*see* client information sheet 4.1). The central treatment targets are therefore:

1. negative beliefs about intrusive thoughts
2. behavioural responses to intrusions
3. worries about the intrusions known as meta-cognitions.

Familiarity and experience with accepted cognitive and behavioural treatments for OCD is recommended before embarking upon modifications which might be necessary for clients with psychosis. Treatments are well described in the literature; the practice manual and conceptual guide to cognitive therapy for the anxiety disorders by Adrian Wells is particularly recommended (Wells, 1997).

Special considerations and modifications in the treatment of OCD in clients with psychosis

> The key to successful OCD treatment with people who have psychosis is thorough knowledge of your client. A full understanding of the meaning of their OC and psychotic symptoms is required. A good formulation is essential in order to accurately predict the likely outcomes of all treatment procedures. If there is potential for techniques to have iatrogenic effects, modify or use a different strategy.

Exposure and response prevention

This is the main treatment procedure in OCD. It works by tackling the maintaining role of rituals and neutralising responses by enabling the client to habituate to the anxiety which is produced on exposure to the feared stimulus. This is essentially a behavioural treatment and when used in the treatment of overt rituals, such as hand washing, the results are observable. It is also possible to use this procedure with internal events such as obsessional thoughts and covert compulsions. However, when used to treat unobservable events, the practice relies on the client providing accurate and reliable self-report. Hence the client must be very motivated and engaged in the therapy before this is attempted. Thought disorder, ideas of reference, paranoid ideation, and limited insight are all likely to reduce the compliance necessary for this procedure.

The procedure can be used in cases where a person fears that they could harm or attack someone, eg this might involve the person handling sharp knives in front of their feared target. However, this procedure is not recommended in cases where clients with psychosis have acted on their urges and/or with clients with forensic histories of significance or co-morbid personality disorder.

Behavioural experiments

Behavioural experiments are designed to challenge beliefs and negative automatic thoughts by demonstrating actual outcomes.

A) Thought suppression experiments

A typical experiment might involve asking the client to try hard not to think of, for example, 'a red cat', for three minutes; the typical outcome is difficulty in suppressing the image or repeated intrusions of the thought.

There are two types of thought suppression experiment: those that demonstrate the effect of thought suppression on thought frequency (it increases!) and those that examine the effect of thought suppression on negative appraisals. Both are appropriate to use with people with psychosis. Careful differentiation between intrusive thoughts and intrusive voices might also be pertinent. The difference is the source to which the person attributes the phenomena: internal attribution of thoughts and external attribution of 'voices'. Behavioural experiments can be very helpful in demonstrating that responses to thoughts significantly influence their frequency and meaning. Increasing self-efficacy can also have beneficial effects on the management and perceived power of voices.

B) Loss of control experiments

Loss of control experiments are used in standard OCD treatment in order to demonstrate that it is not possible to force oneself to lose control even if one tries very hard to do so. Paradoxical techniques also include trying to lose control of one's mind or behaviour. This type of approach should be used with caution with people who have experienced actual loss of control when psychotic and is only suitable for clients in remission who are not currently experiencing distressing psychotic symptoms. Even under these circumstances such a task could be frightening and if there is any doubt regarding the likely outcome, this type of experiment is best avoided.

C) 'Pushing limits'

This type of experiment is another paradoxical technique in which the client is invited to deliberately increase their catastrophic thoughts by thinking beyond even their worst fears in situations where they fear catastrophe could strike. This is not recommended for clients whose fears are related to psychotic intrusions or personal traumas.

D) Controlled worry experiment

This strategy is designed to show that worry can be controlled and that worry is not dangerous; clients learn that they can postpone their worry to their designated 'worry period' (this period is then only used if felt necessary at the time). Clients with psychosis who have beliefs such as 'failure to control worry can lead to psychotic relapse', are only likely to be able to use this strategy following weakening of the belief by verbal reattribution.

Verbal reattribution

There are several ways in which meta-worries and associated negative beliefs can be modified by discussion using Socratic questioning.

A) Questioning the evidence

This is a process in which the therapist elicits the evidence for the worry and, if possible, evidence against the worry. In this way the client comes to challenge the validity of their own worries and beliefs. However, worries frequently include fears of 'going mad' or 'acting crazy'. For people who have experienced an episode of psychosis this fear might be realistic. Therefore, instead of disputing the evidence, questions designed to elicit the person's relapse signature and known early warning signs for relapse can be used to compare and contrast OC intrusions with relapse indicators.

B) Questioning the mechanism

This is another way of reducing the misperception that worry can lead to a feared outcome. Being unable to find a causal mechanism can help to diminish the worry. However, in people with psychosis, the mechanism might have some validity. For example, the fear that increased stress might cause an increased vulnerability to relapse is accurate. In such cases exploration of the intricacies of the relationship between stress and relapse in their specific case is likely to reveal a multi-factorial mechanism rather than a direct link. Chapter 1 examines the model of stress in psychosis.

C) Normalisation of intrusions

This is often used to demonstrate that the majority of people frequently worry: it is not abnormal to worry, nor is it damaging or indicative of mental illness. Often clients are invited to conduct mini-surveys of family and friends in order to reinforce this concept. Normalising intrusions can be helpful in showing that their worrying thoughts are not necessarily due to the psychosis. Therapist presentation of data on prevalence of worry and negative thoughts might be preferred to surveys if those surveyed are likely to hold preconceived ideas about psychosis and confirm an erroneous belief that all symptoms are linked to psychosis.

D) Dissonance techniques

Dissonance techniques can help to demonstrate illogical beliefs. Often the person holds both positive beliefs about worry, eg 'worry keeps me safe' and negative beliefs, eg 'worry is harming me'. Socratic questioning can weaken one or sometimes both of the competing beliefs. This technique can be used successfully with people with psychosis if the beliefs are likely to be amenable to such challenge. Success is less likely with strongly held beliefs, overvalued ideas and magical thinking.

Testing specific beliefs

Common cognitive biases in OCD such as thought-action fusion and thought-event fusion can be tested by techniques in which the person tries to cause a negative action or event by willing it to happen. This technique is the equivalent of exposure and response prevention, ie the person is instructed to increase their intrusions while abandoning neutralising rituals. Careful consideration is needed when setting up such tests with clients who experience fixed delusional beliefs of omnipotence – especially beliefs of causing disasters or harm. However, this procedure can be very beneficial in cases where the person is able to confront such fears and test them out in a controlled manner. For example, a man who was very distressed by the belief that he had caused a plane to crash was compelled to perform counteracting rituals whenever a plane flew overhead (repeating a prayer 20 times in order to keep the plane flying). He was successful in diminishing this belief by gradually reducing and then stopping his prayer; eventually he was able to try to make planes fall from the sky. Subsequently the delusional belief that he had caused a plane to crash diminished and with it the guilt and anxiety which he had experienced.

Questioning the *mechanism* in thought-action fusion can be very helpful in loosening the belief that thinking something bad can cause it to happen. Asking how thinking a thought can cause an action might reveal belief in an irrational mechanism, eg psychic powers or brain waves, in which case behavioural experiments to test the powers can be designed.

Questioning the *incongruence* of thought-action fusion should be used judiciously, eg the question 'What sort of person is likely to act on a negative thought?' is designed to show that the person is very different from one whom they would imagine acting on a harmful thought. However, if the answer is likely to be 'a person with psychosis' or is congruent with a delusional belief, eg 'someone who is evil' or 'those tempted by the devil' this technique is not likely to be helpful. In this case such beliefs should be addressed first.

Dysfunctional thought records and other 'between-sessions' assignments

Clients treated for OCD are invited to routinely monitor their intrusive thoughts and responses to them using the eight-column dysfunctional thought record (*see* Wells (1997)). This makes it possible to practise distinguishing between intrusive thoughts and meta-cognition (worries about the thoughts) as well as providing practice in challenging the thoughts and recognising emotional and other responses. It is therefore a very powerful tool in CBT for OCD. Clients with psychosis can find this task very demanding due to problems with attention and concentration, the sedative effects of medication, difficulty separating intrusive thoughts from meta-cognitions and voices and interference from psychotic symptoms. It is often helpful therefore to complete simple records with the client in session. Initially these can be aimed at eliciting intrusive thoughts and their associated emotional responses. Gradual addition of columns such as: 'worry about the intrusion' / 'answer to worry' / 'emotion' can be made once success has been achieved with the simplified versions. Between-sessions assignments should only be set once the client is fully able to complete the task on their own.

Mindfulness

The practice of 'detached mindfulness' develops the ability to not engage with intrusions. Although sometimes described as merely a technique to reduce the distress caused by intrusions, mindfulness can be a very important element in the treatment of OCD in psychosis. In addition to learning to 'let go' of intrusions when they occur, clients can be taught to develop mindfulness in everyday life with formal periods of mindfulness practice. Mindfulness can produce a number of beneficial effects:

- It can help the person to disengage from the intrusions and therefore reduce rumination and the use of neutralising.
- The client experiences 'in vivo' that it is their responses to the intrusions rather than the intrusions per se that causes them distress.
- The realisation that the feared consequences do not materialise when they do not engage in neutralising rituals often also has beneficial effects in relation to auditory hallucinations. The fear of reprisal or negative consequences for not attending to voices or obeying command hallucinations often mirrors OC fears. Reducing the perceived power of the thoughts can have a consequent diminution on the power of voices.
- Mindfulness helps the client to develop a different relationship with their intrusions. They might become able to bring awareness to them, see them for what they are and let them go: identify, label (eg 'this is a thought, not a fact') and release. This helps to reduce the salience of the thoughts as they are viewed as 'just thoughts' and therefore personal significance is diminished. The same process can be employed with voices and other psychotic symptoms.

If you don't take the thoughts personally they won't take you personally.

Jon Kabat-Zinn

CLIENT INFORMATION SHEET 4.1 – OBSESSIONAL COMPULSIVE DISORDER

What is OCD?

Obsessional Compulsive Disorder, known as OCD, is an anxiety disorder. It affects approximately 2.5 per cent of the general population at some point in their life. In people with psychosis it is even more common: approximately 15 per cent of people with psychosis are likely to experience significant OC symptoms at some time.

A person with OCD experiences intrusive obsessions and/or compulsions that are time consuming, ie take up more than one hour per day. These symptoms are distressing and/or interfere with daily life.

Common symptoms

Obsessions are persistent repetitive thoughts, images or impulses. They are experienced as intrusive, disturbing and difficult to control. They are different from common repetitive thoughts that everyone has from time to time because they tend to be more intense, persistent and distressing.

Obsessions can take the form of visual images, eg of a distressing scene or picturing oneself acting in an inappropriate way. They can also be experienced as impulses such as an urge to act in an improper, unacceptable or dangerous way.

Common obsessions include thoughts, images and urges related to:

- contamination, eg germs, poison
- doubting, eg worries about leaving on electrical items or doors unlocked
- aggression or harm, eg urges to harm others or fears that one might have injured others
- sexual matters, eg images of unacceptable behaviour or repetitive thoughts about one's sexuality
- physical health, eg persistent worries about unusual symptoms
- blasphemy, eg urges to swear or shout out in church.

Compulsions or rituals are repetitive behaviours. They might be carried out in one's head such as praying, counting, or repeating words or phrases; these are known as 'covert' compulsions. Behaviour such as hand washing, checking, ordering or aligning objects and cleaning are known as overt rituals because they are able to be seen. Sometimes both occur together, eg repeatedly turning a tap on and off while counting to a certain number.

What causes OCD?

The perception of a threatening consequence to one's thoughts transforms normal thoughts into obsessional intrusions.

Rassin

It is the *meaning* that a person gives to the thoughts, image or urge that creates distress, not the thought itself. The personal meaning or *significance* that is given to such thoughts increases their power and creates anxiety and worry. Typically there are three ways in which people with OCD tend to interpret their thoughts images and urges:

- Thinking about an unacceptable or disturbing event makes it more likely to happen (known as likelihood thought-action fusion).
- Thinking something bad is as bad as doing it (known as moral equivalence thought-action fusion).
- Thinking that things are possible even when they are scientifically impossible (known as magical thinking).

People who develop OCD often have particular characteristics and beliefs, such as:

- being superstitious
- feeling personally responsible for things that are outside their control (inflated responsibility)
- setting very high standards or rules (perfectionism)
- a tendency to predict the worst possible outcome in neutral or even positive situations (catastrophic misinterpretation)
- a tendency to find personal meaning and significance in events (salience).

Some of these tendencies are also typical in people who have psychosis, which is probably why OCD is so common in psychosis.

Understanding OCD

There is a relationship between one's beliefs, thoughts, emotions and behaviour.

In OCD a particular pattern is established which starts up a 'vicious cycle' in which a person can become trapped:

1. A trigger starts off this pattern. It could be a thought, a doubt or an emotion. For example, 'Hurt your child'.
2. This triggers a belief about the thought. Such beliefs are usually the type of

beliefs described above such as thought-action fusion beliefs. For example, 'Thinking that I could hurt my child makes it more likely that I will'.

3. The belief, in turn, is interpreted; usually this is a catastrophic misinterpretation. For example, 'This is a very dangerous thought, I must be a dangerous person'.
4. The response to this thought is to try to get rid of it or 'neutralise' it; to make it OK. This leads to compulsions or rituals which are behaviours designed to reduce anxiety but, as we shall see, actually make the problem worse in the long run, eg counting, or repeating a phrase such as 'don't do it' for a period of time.
5. Beliefs about the ritual strengthen the original belief. For example, 'If I don't neutralise this thought I will act it out' or 'If I successfully complete my repetitions I will make myself safe'. This makes it more likely that a pattern will be set up and so the vicious cycle develops.
6. All these worrying thoughts create anxiety symptoms and other emotional responses. These in turn add to the distress caused because they are also interpreted as meaningful rather than just seen as what they are: symptoms of anxiety. For example, palpitations, sweating or shaking can be interpreted as signs of losing control; eg 'My heart is racing I could lose control and hurt my child'.

Treatment for OCD

It is the mark of an educated mind to be able to entertain a thought without accepting it.

Aristotle

Treatment is aimed at breaking the vicious cycle that is triggered by the intrusive thought, image or urge. The aim of treatment is not to get rid of the trigger but to tackle the beliefs which create the anxiety and fuel the 'vicious cycle'.

The main treatment approach is called 'exposure with response prevention'. This basically works by experiencing the feared trigger without engaging in the usual 'neutralising' behaviour until the anxiety passes. The experience shows that nothing bad happens and this weakens the belief. For example, someone with a fear of stabbing would hold a knife while resisting any compulsion to go through their usual ritual. Although anxiety is experienced it does pass.

There are many other experiments which help to weaken the beliefs that drive OCD.

Other treatments involve techniques such as:

- looking at evidence for and against beliefs
- examining scientifically how something can be caused by something else
- testing specific beliefs
- learning ways to 'detach' from the thoughts and let them go.

Worry gives a small thing a big shadow.

Swedish proverb

5 Post-traumatic stress disorder and psychosis

Post-traumatic stress disorder (PTSD) is an anxiety disorder which can develop after exposure to any event in which the person experienced intense fear, helplessness or horror. There are very many possible traumatic stressors which can be experienced or witnessed and which may involve actual or threatened death or serious injury or a threat to the physical integrity of self or others. It has been argued (eg Brewin *et al*, 2009) that a diagnosis of PTSD should not be reliant on the presence of an identified trauma or on the person's perceived reactions to the trauma. Instead they assert that clinicians should focus solely on symptomatic presentation and the most appropriate treatment. Lifetime prevalence for PTSD in the general population is estimated to be approximately 8 per cent.

TABLE 5.1 Symptoms of PTSD

Symptom cluster	Example
Re-experiencing	• recurrent distressing dreams of the event • repeated distressing images of the event • feeling or acting as if the event were occurring • 'flashbacks', illusions, hallucinations of the event • intense psychological distress/reactivity when exposed to cues or triggers related to the event
Avoidance	• efforts to avoid external reminders of the trauma including conversations, situations, places • efforts to avoid internal reminders such as thoughts, feelings, emotions associated with the trauma
Numbing	• inability to recall aspects of the event • feelings of detachment • dissociation • restricted range of affect
Hyper-arousal	• hypervigilance • exaggerated startle response • sleep disturbance

Symptoms of PTSD

There is a wide range of PTSD reactions. The major symptom clusters and specific examples are shown in Table 5.1 (on previous page).

Prevalence and significance of PTSD in psychosis

The prevalence and understanding of PTSD within psychosis is an area that has received little systematic evaluation. Consequently, data on people with a dual diagnosis of PTSD and psychoses are limited (Soraya *et al*, 2003). Clinicians do not routinely screen for psychotic symptoms in patients with PTSD and tend not to consider a diagnosis of PTSD in patients with psychosis. Estimates of the prevalence of PTSD in people with psychosis vary greatly depending on the particular cohort studied, eg a 26.5 per cent prevalence of PTSD was found in people with trauma exposure on their first psychiatric admission with psychosis (Neria *et al*, 2002). A group of people recovering from an acute psychotic episode within two to three years of onset of their illness were assessed as in-patients and followed up on two occasions during the year after discharge. The prevalence of PTSD in this group was found to be 46 per cent at 4 months and 35 per cent at 11 months (McGorry *et al*, 1991). It seems likely that on average approximately one in three people with psychosis would fulfil the diagnostic criteria for PTSD at any one time.

People with a diagnosis of both psychosis and PTSD are likely to have higher use of healthcare, elevated levels of psychotic symptoms, higher prevalence of drug and alcohol misuse, are at increased risk of suicide, and have poorer quality of life than those with psychosis alone (Mueser *et al*, 2002).

In a study which investigated associations between specific traumas and psychotic symptoms, Kilcommons and Morrison (2005) found that severity of trauma was associated with severity of PTSD and psychotic experiences. Physical abuse was associated with positive psychotic symptoms and sexual abuse was specifically related to hallucinations. Dissociative processes and negative beliefs formed as a result of trauma were found to be associated with psychotic experiences, particularly hallucinations. The prevalence of post-traumatic stress disorder in their sample of people with psychosis was found to be 53 per cent.

Relationship between trauma and psychosis

The exact relationship between trauma and psychosis varies across individuals and an individualised formulation is required to fully address the impact and significance of trauma in a person with psychosis. It has been proposed that 'traumatic psychosis' exists as a clinical subgroup of schizophrenia; the other subgroups being: sensitivity psychosis, drug-related psychosis and anxiety psychosis (Kingdon and Turkington, 2005). In this classification typical features of traumatic psychosis include malevolent auditory hallucinations, particularly second-person abusive voices and command hallucinations, which are experienced as shocking and alien, tend to be repetitive and distressing and with a tendency to self-blame. Traumatic psychosis, especially as a result of sexual abuse, is associated with PTSD, with depression, and suicidal thoughts. Kingdon and Turkington (2005) suggest that there is a significant overlap with borderline personality disorder.

As in the case of other co-morbid disorders, it is helpful to look at the development of PTSD in relation to one of three possible core pathways.

1) PTSD as a consequence of psychosis

A psychotic episode is itself frequently experienced as a traumatic event. A psychotic episode has many characteristics which would 'qualify' as a trauma in the diagnosis of PTSD:

- Internal events can share the same trauma characteristics as external events and thus be experienced as equally distressing. The characteristics which contribute to the experience of an event as traumatic include: intensity, severity, duration, unexpectedness, perceptions of control and cultural/symbolic aspects (Foy *et al*, 1984). Psychotic episodes are commonly experienced as intense, severe; can last for days or weeks; are often sudden; experienced as completely beyond the person's control and usually have extreme salience. The episode is experienced as real and as external to the individual.
- Terrifying hallucinations and/or delusional beliefs can have a severe impact on a person's view of themself, the world and others (cf Bayley (1996)).
- The psychotic episode can be 're-lived' even in remission and can be experienced as a flashback including the cognitive, sensory and affective experience.
- Clients often describe attempts to avoid cognitive, affective and situational reminders of the psychotic episode (Shaner and Eth, 1989).
- Psychotic experiences frequently evoke the same intense fear, helplessness and horror as do external traumas.
- Threat is commonly a major theme in delusions and hallucinations. Acute psychotic episodes are often experienced as threatening to life (one's own or others'), or to physical integrity. Examples include: that the world is about to end; that one's family is in imminent danger; that oneself or one's family is being killed, tortured, or raped.

In addition to the direct experience of a traumatic psychotic episode, PTSD could be indirectly caused by the experiences which commonly follow an acute psychotic episode – particularly the first episode. Several factors are likely to contribute to the experience of trauma in this circumstance. First, acute loss: loss of employment, loss of control over one's life, estrangement from friends and family. Second, this crisis occurs at a time of limited personal resources due to the psychosis and perhaps precipitating cumulative stressors. Third, the person's previous existence and environment might be altered for a significant period of time; some may never be able to return to their former life circumstances. The ratio of loss to available resources and potential for prolonged alteration of the post trauma environment are characteristics which contribute to the experience of traumatic stress (Foy *et al*, 1984).

Potential contributors to the formation of post-traumatic stress reactions in people with psychosis are shown in Box 5.1.

Box 5.1 Potential indirect contributory factors to the development of PTSD following a psychotic episode

- The experience of being made subject to mental health legislation.
- Perception of being betrayed by and/or estranged from family/friends.
- Loss of education or employment.
- Separation from usual supports and positive experiences.
- Enforced hospitalisation (voluntary hospitalisation, while less likely to be experienced as traumatic, still involves a loss of familiar environment and control at a time of acute crisis and confusion).
- Enforced medication (this can involve being forcibly restrained and injected against one's will).
- Witnessing extreme behaviours in other in-patients, including aggression, sexual disinhibition, screaming.
- Experience or witnessing of physical restraint, sedation, seclusion.
- Forensic and/or legal repercussions of behaviour while acutely psychotic, eg threatened or actual harm to others.
- Consequences of parasuicidal behaviour whilst psychotic, ie attempts to harm or kill self.

2) Psychosis as a consequence of trauma

The emergence of psychosis as a result of trauma is generally described in relation to traumatic life events which were experienced prior to the onset of psychosis – often many years earlier. The frequency of trauma in the lives of people with psychosis is well documented. Studies of trauma in the early lives of people who subsequently develop psychosis tend to give estimates of between 70 per cent and 98 per cent (eg Mueser *et al*, 1998).

Data from the second British National Survey of Psychiatric Morbidity found that of people with psychosis, 34.5 per cent were victims of sexual abuse, 46.4 per cent experienced bullying and 38.1 per cent experienced violence in the home

(Bebbington *et al*, 2004). A prospective study of people in the general population found that reported sexual abuse was a predictor of subsequent development of positive psychotic symptoms; an odds ratio of 11.5 was found for severe abuse (Janssen *et al*, 2004).

Experience of trauma does not, of course, imply that the person would meet criteria for a diagnosis of PTSD. The evidence suggests that exposure to trauma does increase the likelihood of developing psychosis in vulnerable individuals and that trauma is a common occurrence for people with a diagnosis of psychosis (Morrison *et al*, 2003).

3) Shared developmental pathway: phenomenological links between symptoms of PTSD and psychosis

There appear to be three primary phenomenological links. First there are some striking similarities between PTSD symptoms and those found in psychosis. These include:

- intrusive thoughts and images
- flashback experiences or reliving which often involve auditory, visual, tactile and/or olfactory phenomena
- paranoid thoughts and reactions
- increased levels of arousal, hypervigilance and sleep disturbance
- negative symptoms such as emotional numbing, social isolation, impaired concentration, affective flattening and anhedonia are typical of both PTSD and psychosis.

Second, vulnerability factors for psychosis are also remarkably similar to those which have been identified as increasing vulnerability to PTSD: lack of social support, childhood abuse, familial psychiatric history, racial minority status, adverse childhood experience, low socio-economic status, poor educational opportunities and schizotypy (Brewin *et al*, 2000).

Third, there are often similarities in content between psychotic symptoms and the trauma experienced. In a community sample of 200 people with psychosis, hallucinations were found to be significantly related to sexual abuse and childhood physical abuse. The relationship was particularly strong for commenting voices and command hallucinations (Read *et al*, 2003). These individuals are similar in presentation to those classified as having 'traumatic psychosis' in the subgroup system of Kingdon and Turkington (2005). A further study of 75 people with psychosis found that 26 per cent met the criteria for PTSD and 55 per cent of the sample reported that their hallucinations related to past stressful life events. Independent researchers found that 30 per cent of the hallucinations had similar themes and 7 per cent had direct similarities to the trauma experienced and were likely to be trauma memories (Hardy *et al*, 2005).

While it is possible that the congruence between the nature and content of symptoms of PTSD and psychosis might indicate a causal link, it is also the case that psychiatric symptoms are often closely related to the person's developmental history. Therefore, if that history contains traumatic experiences they are likely to feature in the person's development of explanations for anomalous experiences such as somatic hallucinations, abusive voices and delusions of abuse (Morrison *et al*, 2003).

Assessment of post-traumatic stress disorder

When assessing for PTSD in psychosis, the single most important procedure is the construction of a trauma history. While administering screening questionnaires can be useful in the identification of potential traumas, it is likely that traumatic experiences may be missed, avoided or simply not recognised as significant by the person.

Box 5.2 Ten-point guide to taking a trauma history

1. Provide an introduction and an explanation of why you will be asking about the person's experience of trauma.
2. Normalise the experience of trauma and explain the common co-occurrence of trauma and mental health problems.
3. Be empathic and compassionate but try not to show excessive concern as this could inhibit further disclosure.
4. Be sensitive but endeavour not to collude in avoidance.
5. Aim to remain unemotional and 'matter-of fact'; clients quickly pick up expressions of shock or disgust.
6. Seek to build a shared understanding of the experience(s) and what they mean to the client.
7. Use a semi-structured interview but be prepared to be flexible and to explore issues in more depth as they arise.
8. Maintain a relaxed and sensitive pace; do not rush.
9. Ensure that there is time at the end of the session to sensitively bring the conversation to an appropriate ending so that the client feels listened to and grounded before they leave.
10. Do not book in a client immediately after such an interview as you might also want some time to process what you have heard.

It is therefore recommended that a full trauma history interview is conducted. This can be potentially difficult for both the client and therapist; a guide to taking a trauma history is presented in Box 5.2.

The assessment process can take many sessions and further assessment, formal and informal, is likely to continue throughout the intervention.

Formal assessment measures

Diagnosis can be assisted by specifically designed scales:

- *Clinician-Administered PTSD Scale for Schizophrenia* (CAPS-S) (Gearon *et al*, 2004)
  This is a useful diagnostic interview scale for the formal assessment of PTSD in psychosis. It is linked to the current DSM-IV-TR diagnostic criteria and based upon the widely used Clinician-Administered PTSD scale known as the CAPS (Blake *et al*, 1995). Although the scale is lengthy and takes time to administer it can lend structure to the trauma history interview and produces detailed information which is helpful in formulation.
- *The Posttraumatic Diagnostic Scale* (PDS) (Foa, 1995)
  This widely used scale provides a detailed trauma checklist and assesses the severity of the DSM IV-TR PTSD symptoms. It is sensitive to treatment change on these criteria and has a short administration time (10 minutes).

Specific issues can be formally assessed using measures to address concerns commonly related to PTSD:

- *The Trauma-Related Guilt Inventory* (TRGI) (Kubany *et al*, 1996)
  This scale assesses cognitive and emotional aspects of guilt associated with specific traumatic events. It has three scales: global guilt, distress, and guilt cognitions which are further divided into hindsight bias and/or responsibility, wrongdoing, and lack of justification.
- *The Dissociative Experiences Scale* (DES) (Bernstein and Putnam, 1986)
  This widely used 28-item self-report scale measures common dissociative experiences. Responses are made by indicating the percentage to which the symptom is experienced. Although originally designed as a screen for dissociative identity disorder it is useful in assessing dissociative symptoms and has good psychometric properties. The DES is presented in the appendix (pp. 141–5).

Other measures to consider:

- Beck Anxiety Inventory (BAI) (Beck *et al*, 1988)
- Beck Depression Inventory (BDI) (Beck *et al*, 1996)
- State–Trait Anger Expression Inventory (Speilberger, 1988)

Working model of trauma and psychosis

Psychological investigation into the human processing of trauma has produced pragmatic theories of the formation of PTSD which have been used to inform psychological treatments. The dual representation theory (Brewin *et al*, 1996; 2010) highlights the importance of the nature of stored memories – sensation-based memory (S-REPS) and contextual memory (C-REPS) being differently stored, organised and accessed. Trauma memories, stored in the amygdala, tend to lack context and have no 'time-tag'; they are not updated, are 'frozen in time', are more fragmented and tend to elicit autonomic responses – hence when they are remembered they are experienced as more vivid and real. Contextual memories stored in the hippocampus are more organised, are integrated with previous knowledge, updated and 'time-tagged'.

Cognitive models of PTSD (eg Ehlers and Clark, 2000) emphasise cognitive processing during the trauma and the nature of trauma memory. In particular, such models suggest that PTSD becomes persistent when the trauma is processed in a way which evokes a sense of serious current threat. The salience of 'current threat' is maintained by 'excessively negative appraisals of the trauma and/or its sequelae and a disturbance of autobiographical memory characterised by poor elaboration and contextualisation, strong associative memory and strong perceptual priming' (Ehlers and Clark, 2000). Negative appraisals are maintained by maladaptive cognitive and behavioural strategies and processing styles.

Morrison *et al*, (2003) have incorporated aspects of cognitive models of both PTSD and psychosis to produce an integrative model of trauma and psychosis. This model can be used to help clients to make sense of their experiences and the role of trauma in the formation and maintenance of symptoms. This approach normalises symptoms and emphasises the developmental and maintaining role of beliefs, and cognitive and behavioural responses. A client in whom PTSD appears to exist as separate from psychosis can be conceptualised and treated as would clients with PTSD alone (eg Taylor, 2006). However, the majority of clients are likely to benefit from an approach informed by the integrated model.

The model is shown in Figure 5.1. The model illustrates how the trauma, or trauma memory, induces post-traumatic intrusions such as flashbacks or re-living, commonly of the worst aspects of the trauma. These are not always accurate representations of the actual event and are not always appraised as PTSD. Indeed, the key to whether the intrusions are regarded as PTSD or as psychotic phenomena is the way in which they are appraised. Hearing verbal abuse which is attributed internally to a vivid memory would be conceptualised as PTSD whereas the same intrusion attributed externally, eg to a malevolent voice, would be likely to be regarded as psychotic. Often the link between a past trauma and subsequent intrusions is not recognised by the client or by health professionals, making the symptom appraisal more likely to be classified as psychotic. Morrison *et al*, (2003)

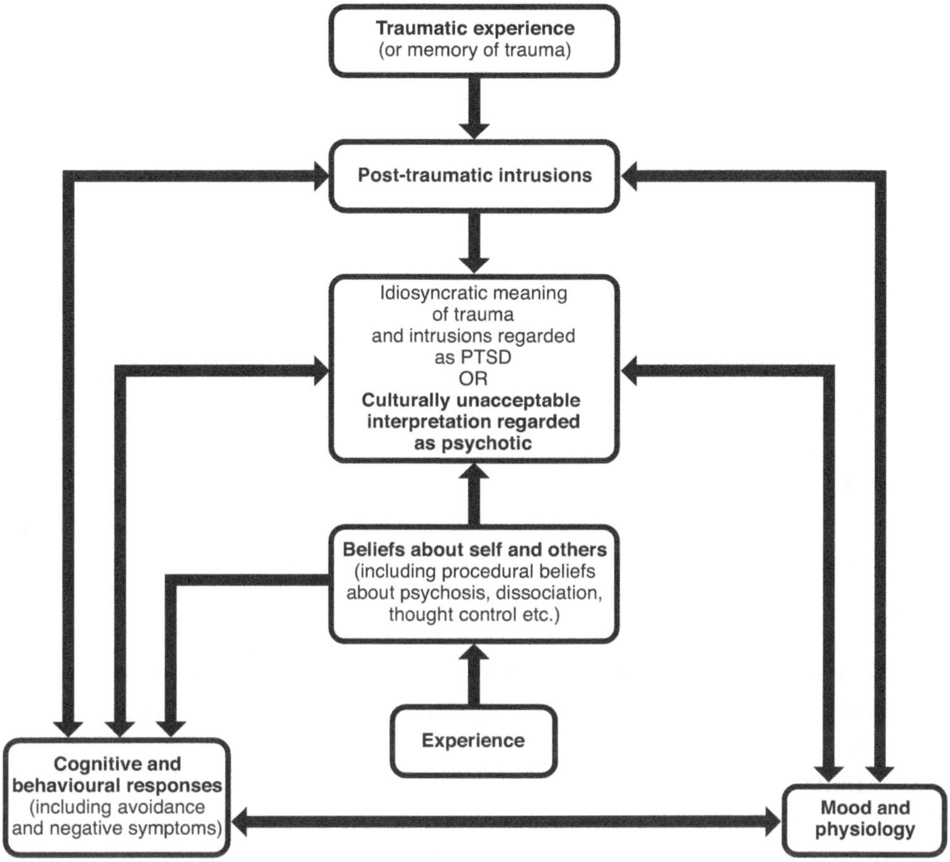

FIGURE 5.1 Integrative model of trauma and psychosis
Reproduced with kind permission from Morrison AP, Frame L and Larkin W (2003) 'Relationships between trauma and psychosis: a review and integration', *British Journal of Clinical Psychology*, 42, pp331–53, Wiley.

point out 'the transparency of the links between symptom content and life events to both the patient and professional may determine which diagnosis is received', and further propose that holding positive beliefs such as 'hearing voices is reassuring and guards against loneliness' might further predispose towards a psychotic explanation. This fits with the notion of psychosis developing as a coping strategy for trauma (Romme and Escher, 1989).

Similarly, cognitive, behavioural, emotional and physiological responses – eg emotional numbing – can be viewed as coping strategies. The person's beliefs about themself and others, based on their life experiences, inform their likely interpretation of their symptom experiences: if they have experienced loss, abuse and neglect as a child they are more likely to see themself as vulnerable and the world as a dangerous and unpredictable place. Dissociation as a strategy for coping with distressing intrusions, particularly if previously experienced during trauma, can contribute to further social dislocation and culturally unacceptable explanations for intrusions, eg racing heart being caused by being 'taken over' by a third party. The model suggests that such explanations are maintained by factors such as social environment, safety behaviours, thought-control strategies and selective attention.

Guide to formulation for trauma in psychosis

Using the integrative model as a guide, a shared formulation can be developed with the client. The key to formulation is making links between events (eg abuse) and experiences (eg intrusions). Development of a shared understanding of the relationship between events and experiences is central to conceptualisation and informs treatment.

Ten key points in formulation for trauma and psychosis are discussed below.

1. If the conceptualisation is clear, formulations might incorporate two or more traumatic experiences, eg childhood physical abuse and adult assault. Indeed, there may be links between the consequences of the traumas which suggest that a shared formulation is appropriate. However, if a person has experienced multiple traumas it is recommended that separate formulations be developed rather than attempting to incorporate everything into one overly complex formulation.
2. Identify the traumatic experience(s) and its/their relevance: not all traumas result in PTSD and apparently less severe traumatic experiences can have greater impact than seemingly more severe ones.
3. Investigate the content and nature of the post-traumatic intrusions. These might be images, voices, or other sensory experiences such as smells, tastes or somatic sensations. These tend to be re-experiences which are experienced as current threat. It might be possible to identify 'matching triggers', ie those cues – internal or external – which can evoke the trauma memory, eg emotional triggers such as fear or physical sensations.
4. Be alert to 'hot-spots'. These are specific aspects of trauma memory that cause high levels of distress. They are usually the person's 'worst moments' and can be difficult to deliberately recall because of the way they are encoded in sensation-based memory. In discussion with clients they can be identified by sudden changes in affect and often by 'gaps' in their narrative, by speeding up or avoidance. Careful exploration of the meaning and significance of such hot-spots can identify potential treatment targets.
5. Explore the interpretation of the intrusions. The explanation is likely to be regarded as psychotic especially if the link between the trauma and the interpretation of experiences is not apparent. The experiences are usually externally

attributed, eg to voices. Delusional beliefs might have developed to explain the persistence of the experiences. Being able to differentiate between re-experiencing, psychotic phenomena and dissociation can provide a powerful way of helping the client to re-attribute their experiences and reduce distress.

6. Examine the person's beliefs about themself and others. These are informed by their life experiences, cultural and social background. A good place to start is by asking the client if any of their beliefs have changed as a result of their traumatic experiences. Beliefs such as 'I am strong' or 'the world is a just place' are often shattered by a traumatic experience. Alternatively, beliefs such as 'people get what they deserve' can lead to the development of negative self-appraisals. Beliefs about the meaning of psychotic interpretations might be protective or have other benefits to the person, eg viewing oneself as special or powerful.
7. Careful exploration of the client's cognitive responses might reveal strategies such as thought suppression.
8. Ask about suicidal ideation.
9. Explore behavioural responses; these might include avoidance, social withdrawal, safety behaviours and checking. Such responses might develop further into suspicious or paranoid behaviour but the origin might be a coping strategy for traumatic intrusions.
10. Assessment of associated emotions, mood and physiological reactions is useful in highlighting a range of possible related issues including depressed mood, guilt, hyper-arousal, sleep disturbance, anger or irritability. Physiological reactions such as sweating or palpitations can reinforce experiences as 'current threat' and set up a vicious cycle of re-experiencing.

CASE VIGNETTE: OSCAR

Oscar is a 31-year-old unemployed man who lives in hostel accommodation. He has had several periods of hospitalisation since age 21 when he experienced an acute psychotic episode in which he believed that he had been buried and resurrected as the son of God. Oscar moved to England from France to live with his aunt when his parents divorced. After six months as a student he dropped out of college and worked in a fast-food restaurant. He struggled to adjust to life in London and started to smoke cannabis. He lost his job and he moved out of his aunt's house to live in a 'squat'. By the age of 20 he was using several illegal drugs. To fund his drug use he started to sell cocaine. A rival drug dealer, who believed that Oscar was encroaching on his territory, arranged to have him kidnapped. He was held in a basement with a sack over his head and his arms tied behind his back for several days. On his release he told no one about his ordeal; his story emerged 10 years later during a trauma history interview for cognitive therapy for psychosis. Oscar had not linked his traumatic experience to his later belief that he had been resurrected. He recalled memories of being 'buried' in a cave and described malevolent voices from Satan. Oscar was diagnosed as having paranoid schizophrenia and had been prescribed antipsychotic medication for 10 years. He intermittently believes that he is being persecuted by Satan because he is the son of God.

A formulation for Oscar is shown in Figure 5.2.

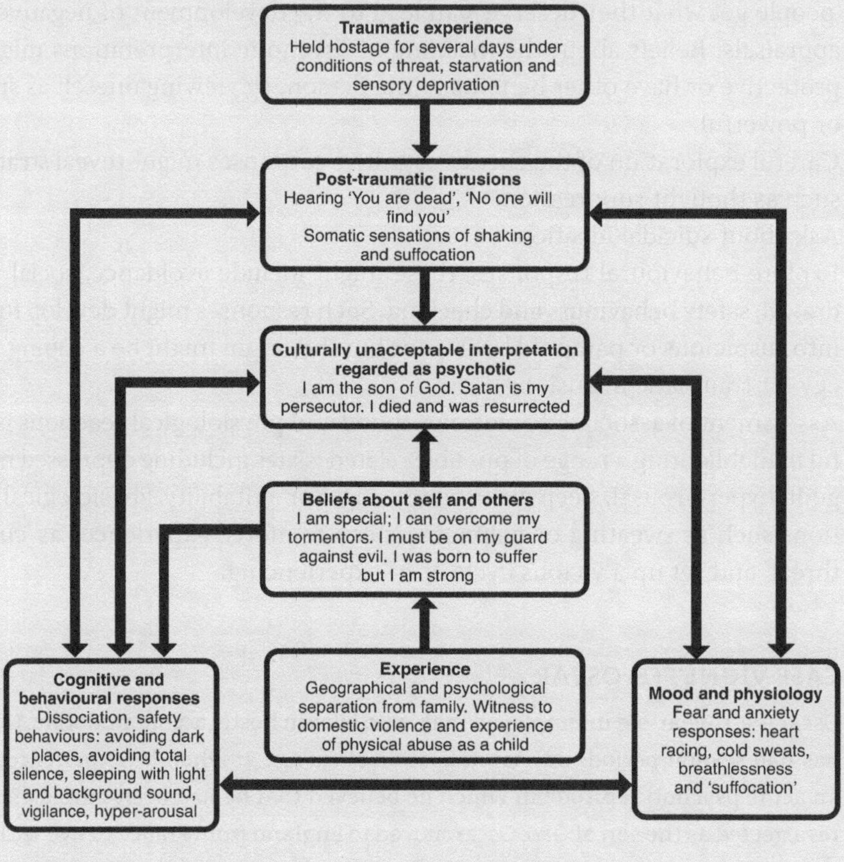

FIGURE 5.2 Formulation PTSD and psychosis: Oscar

Careful documentation of Oscar's personal and trauma history revealed a childhood characterised by unpredictability: violent parental arguments, witnessing of his father physically assaulting his mother from age 5 and experience of numerous parental separations and reunions. Oscar learned to 'stay out of sight' during the violence perpetrated by his father; on occasions when he did try to intervene he was also beaten. His mother treated him well and often referred to him as 'mon garçon spécial', 'my special boy'. As a child Oscar tended to cope by avoidance and by pretending that 'everything was OK'. His descriptions of beatings suggest that he dissociated during physical abuse by his father.

Guilt at 'allowing' his mother to be beaten, and later of leaving her in order to come to England, was also an important component. This was compounded by his shame at dropping out of education and his use of drugs – initially to feel good and later to 'stop feeling'.

Interestingly, Oscar had suppressed the trauma of his kidnap and had not considered this to be important in his subsequent experiences such as hearing voices and somatic symptoms. However, careful questioning about the event revealed a number of links between his experience and his symptoms including likely matching triggers such as emotional triggers – fear and anxiety; physiological triggers – extreme thirst or hunger, and physical triggers – silence and total darkness.

Oscar's belief that he was resurrected as the son of God can be seen as protective against the reality of the trauma, ie a much more positive and potent belief than 'I am a victim of kidnap and abuse by drug dealers'. Guarding against feelings of helplessness also appeared to be important: feeling helpless in the assaults on his mother and himself as a child being mirrored in the helplessness of being held captive. His belief 'I am invincible because I am special' seemed to allow Oscar to accept and rise above his experiences of helplessness by believing that he would always survive. His belief also offered him a sense of being special, as his mother fondly described him, which helped him to cope with the difficult social environment in which he lived. Safety behaviours such as avoidance of dark places and of total silence, as well as vigilance and hyper-arousal maintained his intrusions and interpretations of them as persecution by Satan.

Particular 'hot-spots' were hearing voices telling him that he was dead and that he was totally alone; it is likely that his captors used such derision during his ordeal. Such intrusions created fear and anxiety reactions including feelings of tightness of breath and sweating which he described as 'suffocation'.

Oscar's treatment goals, intervention and outcomes

Following the development of the formulation and psycho-education about the effects of trauma, Oscar was invited to draw up a list of what he would like to achieve in treatment. Three things were important to him: being able to let down his guard so that he could socialise more easily, being less stressed by voices and sleeping better. It was felt that it was not appropriate to directly address the delusional beliefs regarding being the son of God but that he might benefit from re-appraising the voices and their meaning from a trauma perspective.

1. Being able to let down my guard safely

Following discussion it transpired that Oscar was frequently 'on guard' and attentive to references which might indicate that people were 'in league' with Satan and this hyper-vigilance increased the likelihood of triggering fear and anxiety responses (matching triggers to trauma) which in turn reinforced his belief that he was being persecuted. A behavioural experiment was designed in which he deliberately evoked thoughts that an imagined person was in league with Satan and monitored his emotional and cognitive responses. He then compared his responses when he imagined that the person was not harmful. This experiment was conducted successfully several times in session. He was later able to switch his thoughts to imagining people as benign in real-life situations, with a consequent significant reduction in fear and in beliefs of persecution.

2. Being less stressed by the voices

Oscar kept a 'voices log' for three weeks in which he recorded when the voices occurred and his responses to them. It appeared that voices mainly occurred at night when he was alone and that occasionally they were experienced at times when he had neglected to eat; it was hypothesised that matching triggers such as darkness, silence and hunger cues might contribute to the experience of hearing voices. In addition, the voices induced anxiety and fear and he tended to respond to the voices by increasing safety behaviours (turning on the lights and radio). Oscar was able to consider the possibility that the voices were not Satan's but were internally generated. Cognitive restructuring helped Oscar to 'entertain doubt' that the voices were not actually real and might be re-appraised as trauma intrusions. Oscar practised grounding techniques in response to voices; he designed grounding cue cards on which he wrote calming phrases: 'I am alive and well', 'I am safe', 'Voices are harmless'. If he did become caught up in voices he used smelling salts to bring him back to the present. Over a period of months of using these techniques, the voices started to diminish and when they did occur he was no longer distressed by them. He also began to tolerate darkness and silence and gradually relinquished his safety behaviours which appeared to be maintaining the trauma intrusions. In this gradual way he was finally able to reappraise the meaning of the voices which subsequently lost their power to induce fear.

3. Being able to sleep better

Psycho-education about the physiological reactions to anxiety, eg heart racing, sweating and breathlessness, helped Oscar to view these symptoms as normal responses to anxious thoughts rather than having meaning beyond this

(eg suffocation and torment by Satan). Oscar practised mindfulness of breathing before going to bed and regularly spent 10–15 minutes per day practising mindfulness meditation exercises. This helped to reduce his general stress levels and also improved his sleep. Oscar's sleep pattern was further improved by his reduced fear of the darkness and silence.

Effectiveness of CBT for PTSD in psychosis

To date, two randomised controlled trials (RCT) have been published investigating CBT for trauma in people with psychosis. One hundred and eight clients with severe mental illness, received 12–16 sessions consisting of psycho-education, breathing re-training and generic cognitive restructuring. This was found to be effective for trauma symptoms, especially severe trauma. Homework completion predicted outcome and change in trauma-related beliefs mediated change in PTSD symptoms (Mueser *et al*, 2008).

Another RCT looked at the effectiveness of a cognitive therapy based recovery intervention in reducing post-psychotic trauma symptoms following a first episode of psychosis. Participants received a maximum of 26 sessions which included engagement and formulation, trauma processing based on exploration of appraisals, psychotic illness appraisals and relapse prevention. The intervention was found to be effective for trauma symptoms but not for depression. An increased effect was found for those with higher trauma scores (Jackson *et al*, 2009).

Treatment for PTSD in psychosis

> *Out of this nettle, danger, we pluck this flower, safety.*
>
> William Shakespeare, *Henry IV Part 1*

There is a variety of CBT approaches and interventions for PTSD (Taylor, 2006).

A background understanding of cognitive therapy of dissociative symptoms, cognitive restructuring and treatment of childhood memories will be helpful before embarking upon the treatment of PTSD in psychosis (eg Arntz and Weertman, 1999; Grey *et al*, 2002; Kennerley, 1996). The majority of PTSD interventions are suitable for clients with psychosis. The particular intervention strategies selected will depend upon the agreed treatment goals and can be modified to suit the client. Interventions to address the agreed treatment aims should consider the client's abilities to benefit from the approaches and the likely outcome and consequences. For example, a treatment aimed at internal re-attribution is not indicated for a client whose external attribution is not causing distress or significantly interfering with their functioning.

Indications and contra-indications for use of trauma-focused interventions such as elaboration and re-scripting are shown in Box 5.3 (Chisholm *et al*, 2010).

Box 5.3 Indications and contra-indications for the use of trauma-focused interventions

Indications

- Clear direct re-experiencing symptoms
- Few specific trauma(s)
- Client makes links between trauma and symptoms
- Problematic direct trauma-related appraisals
- Client able to use coping strategies to manage own affect and distress
- Use after successful cognitive re-structuring management of hot-spots and change in trauma-related appraisals

Contra-indications

- Client experiencing acute positive symptoms (focus on these first)
- High levels of substance misuse
- Lack of support outside sessions (social or team)
- High risk of self-harm (development of distress tolerance first)
- Immovable entrenched negative schemas

Always gain client understanding and agreement before use of these interventions.

Compilation of a list of desired treatment outcomes will make it possible to focus on the client's goals (eg *see* Oscar's treatment goals).

Primary therapy aim and objectives

The most common aim in the treatment of trauma in psychosis is the reduction of distress. This might be achieved in a number of ways.

1. Use of the formulation to develop the client's understanding of the role of traumatic experience(s) in their psychotic symptoms and how these might be maintained by current coping strategies such as avoidance.
2. Development of new ways of coping with symptoms and with trauma intrusions.
3. Making sense of psychotic symptoms in terms of understandable psychological processes can lead to the client's re-attribution of symptoms to an internal source.

4. Re-appraising the meaning of the trauma(s) and the development of an alternative less distressing understanding or personal narrative.
5. Corrective learning experiences can be provided by cognitive restructuring and/or exposure. These help to create alternative updated memories which reduce the triggering of the 'current threat' association and thereby reduce distress. Exposure does not have to be direct situational exposure; indeed, this is not recommended in clients with psychosis. Talking about the trauma is, in itself, exposure.
6. An alternative autobiographical memory so created will be encoded as a conceptual memory and therefore be more coherent, integrated, voluntary and located in the past; this will then impede the retrieval of the competing sensory PTSD memory.

Treatment interventions

1) Providing a rationale for treatment or psycho-education

Sharing the key concepts of PTSD formation and teaching clients about the common symptoms or experiences can be very helpful in developing a basis for the interventions to follow. The rationale provides normalising explanations for the clients' symptoms/experiences as well as instilling hope that treatment change is possible (*see* client information sheet 5.1).

2) Coping skills enhancement and stabilisation

This should include consideration of risks such as self-harm along with ways of establishing safety during periods of distress. The addition of mild tranquilisers and/or sleeping tablets might be helpful for some people during treatment although stronger sedation can impede the processing of conceptual memory and should be avoided.

Emotion regulation skills such as mindfulness, controlled breathing and relaxation techniques can be taught and practised in session until the client is confident in using such techniques.

Grounding techniques which help to re-establish present-moment reality can be particularly useful for coping with experiences such as dissociation, flashbacks and nightmares. Grounding techniques are described in Box 5.4.

An excellent source of therapeutic techniques related to trauma is: *The Body Remembers: The Psychophysiology of Trauma and Trauma Treatment*, by Babette Rothschild (2000).

This type of work should not be undertaken in isolation. Good liaison with clinical teams is important to ensure that other support is available if needed. Agreeing a crisis plan is also recommended. Such a plan should detail whom to contact should the client require help (eg suicidal ideation).

Box 5.4 Grounding techniques for flashbacks, dissociation and waking from nightmares (Chisholm *et al*, 2010)

1. Environmental focus: concentrate on the immediate environment, eg the colour of the walls, the texture of one's clothing, the feel of the breeze, the sound of people, cars, etc.
2. Grounding object: find a personal 'grounding object' which can be carried and used to bring one back to the present moment. A comforting tangible object that feels pleasant and perhaps has some personal significance, eg a small soft toy or a stress ball would work well.
3. Grounding phrase: develop a self-soothing phrase to bring to mind to calm and return to oneself, eg 'I am safe now', 'everything is cool', 'I'm glad I am here'.
4. Olfactory grounding: a quick and powerful way to bring one back to the present is to briefly inhale a strong scent. Smelling salts are effective as are more calming scents such as lavender. Smell is good at impeding competing sensory and cognitive experiences so it is particularly helpful for flashbacks.
5. Grounding image: bring to mind a calm and peaceful image; this could be a place of personal significance or a 'safe place' that has been practised and rehearsed. Alternatively, bring to mind a soothing word such as 'calm'. Develop the image – vary its size, or the shape, colour and texture of the letters until it feels just right.
6. Distraction: counting in threes, playing a game on a mobile phone, singing along to the radio.

3) Trauma-focused interventions

> *It is always in the midst, in the epicentre, of your troubles that you find serenity.*
>
> Antoine de Saint-Exupery

> *It is helpful to teach clients how to cope with symptoms and experiences as they arise. Any opportunity to understand a symptom and to enhance coping should be utilised.*

Coping with flashbacks

If a client experiences flashbacks it is likely that this will happen during sessions. If the client suddenly appears lost in thought, is unresponsive or looks fearful or dazed it is likely that they are experiencing a flashback. Try to gain their attention by speaking their name softly and repeatedly and then bring them back to the present by using grounding techniques. Remind them where they are and that they are safe. Investigate what triggered the flashback; this will provide useful information to increase awareness of early signs and matching triggers as well as the opportunity to practise how to cope with them.

Identifying and defusing matching triggers for trauma intrusions

Triggers can occur in all sensory modalities: smell, touch, taste, hearing and seeing as well as from internal states such as fear or anxiety and from situations. To allow 'updating' from the original trauma it is useful to explore what is the same and what is different about the original and current triggers. This breaks the link between the stimulus and the trauma memory. Every time the client talks about the trauma they are forming a more integrated conceptual memory; it is likely that more details will emerge and tolerance will increase.

Cognitive restructuring of trauma-related appraisals

Thoughts and emotions regarding the trauma have a significant impact on the ability to recover. Changing one's appraisals can therefore have a dramatic effect in reducing associated distress. Common problems include guilt, shame and anger.

Box 5.5 Cognitive restructuring of trauma-related appraisals

- Examination of 'hindsight bias', eg looking back with knowledge that one did not have at the time. In particular with childhood experiences the person might be encouraged to recall more accurately their physical size and power relationship in regard to an abuser.
- Remembering the actual circumstances rather than 'what if' scenarios.
- Examination of responsibility; placing it where it should be, awareness of tendency towards inflated sense of responsibility.
- Thinking errors; particularly all-or-nothing thinking, personalising, overgeneralising
- Normalising the human fear response; fight, flight or freeze.
- Physiological reactions, eg sexual arousal can occur during rape – this does not mean it was wanted or enjoyed; asking about this can normalise the biological response and eradicate feelings of shame.
- Break the secrecy (abuse). Secrecy is often instilled or demanded by an abuser. This can set up feelings of collusion with the perpetrator and/or of being under their power. Breaking the secrecy can give back a sense of control and reduce the influence of the abuser.
- Compassion and self-forgiveness, eg compassionate mind training (Gilbert 2007).
- Schema-focused interventions to explore underlying core beliefs.

Guilt-related appraisals might include: 'I should have done more', 'I survived and others died', 'It was my fault'. Shame is often maintained by beliefs such as 'I did not fight back', 'I am a coward', 'I am damaged'. Anger appraisals include 'I will get him back', 'How dare they do that to me?', 'She will pay'.

Methods of cognitive restructuring are presented in Box 5.5.

Elaborating the trauma memory

Elaboration is a form of exposure which reduces avoidance and helps the client to reappraise the meaning of the trauma. In PTSD a vicious cycle is established: the trauma is re-experienced as a current threat and the associated emotions can feel overwhelming; this leads to attempts to avoid the intrusions and to further distress which feeds the avoidance; the sensory fragmented memory does not get updated and continues to activate current threat. Exposure to the trauma memory by talking through it in detail will re-organise the memory into an integrated form. This

Box 5.6 Elaborating the trauma memory

- Encourage gentle disclosure.
- Explore obstacles to detailed disclosure, eg 'I will be overwhelmed', 'You will be shocked', 'You will be disgusted'.
- Sometimes a lesser trauma can be elaborated to show that the client can cope and that the approach is effective.
- If the memory is very fragmented and difficult to recall try to find 'anchor points' or draw up a time-line to build up the memory and help to contextualise it.
- If verbalising the trauma is extremely difficult, other forms of expression can be used to build the narrative such as drawing and painting or written accounts. Whatever form is chosen, it should be undertaken in session rather than set as homework in order to provide support and guidance and to be alert to 'hotspots' and/or dissociation.
- Identify and restructure emotional 'hotspots'. This involves identifying the worst moments and the associated emotions, cognitions and meanings. It enables updating and modification of the associated meaning. *See* Grey *et al* (2002) for a comprehensive account of cognitive restructuring of emotional 'hotspots'.
- Emotional hotspots can be addressed in a graded hierarchical way rather than re-living the whole event. Updates should be discussed (eg 'You thought you were going to die but you survived') and practised until the client feels confident with them. If appropriate, the updates can then be inserted into re-living.

rationale requires careful explanation in order to prepare the client who is likely to be reluctant to think about something which they have spent much effort avoiding.

A guide to the elaboration approach is shown in Box 5.6.

Re-scripting using guided imagery transformation

This approach also uses elaboration and updating with the aim of creating new memories so that when the sensory memory is triggered the new memory is activated which impedes the trauma memory. Spontaneous retrieval of positive sensations and emotions has been reported (Brewin *et al*, 2010).

Re-scripting is useful for visual hallucinations, intrusions and flashbacks; it is a way of gaining control over the image.

It involves three steps:

1. The client focuses on the intrusion or image.
2. The therapist guides the client in the construction of an alternative image; it can be as outlandish as imagination allows; it is their creation, they can visualise anything they want to. Ideas include diminishing the aggressor, making them look ridiculous, eg make them unusual colours, change the size or shape of perpetrators and objects, eg a gun could become a banana. Add protective people or objects or even superhuman powers. End on success, eg flying away.
3. The new positive image is rehearsed and modified until it feels strong and affirmative.

A specific type of re-scripting often used with survivors of childhood sexual abuse with PTSD is known as imagery re-scripting and reprocessing therapy (IRRT). A treatment manual is available (Smucker, 2005).

Schema-focused cognitive therapy (SFCT)

SFCT (eg Padesky, 1994; Young *et al*, 2003) aims to modify fixed core beliefs and is indicated when pre-traumatic appraisals appear to be contributing to distress. Schemas such as 'the world is a dangerous and unpredictable place' are likely to have been reinforced by traumatic experiences and can perpetuate trauma intrusions. SFCT can build positive beliefs, challenge specific instances and identify examples of 'self-prejudice'. Shame is commonly a feature of trauma and is perpetuated by underlying core beliefs about oneself and the world. Compassionate mind training is particularly helpful in this regard (eg Lee, 2005).

Relinquishment of maintaining cognitive and behavioural strategies

The integrated model proposes that behavioural and cognitive strategies such as avoidance, thought suppression, rumination and safety behaviours serve to maintain post-traumatic intrusions and their appraisals. Identification of such strategies and examination of their maintenance role can help to persuade the client that giving up such attempts at coping will be beneficial. Behavioural experiments which test out the strategies are effective at producing evidence of their hindrance.

CLIENT INFORMATION SHEET 5.1 – POST-TRAUMATIC STRESS DISORDER (PTSD)

Post-traumatic stress disorder (PTSD) is an anxiety disorder which can develop after experiencing a traumatic event – sometimes many years later. Many people with a diagnosis of psychosis have experienced a traumatic event such as abuse as a child or assault as an adult. Often the experience of one's first acute psychotic episode can be very traumatic. Approximately one in three people with psychosis might have PTSD.

How PTSD develops

Not all traumas lead to PTSD; it seems that the way in which the brain processes the event at the time can lead to problems later on. Sometimes no PTSD symptoms develop until they are triggered by something else, perhaps another trauma or a reminder of the event.

When we experience extreme distress, the traumatic event is not processed and remembered in the same way as other experiences. This is because we go into 'survival mode' and shut down our usual ways of processing information in order to deal with the immediate threat. When this happens the memory of the event is stored in a different part of the brain and has different characteristics from normal memories; this leads to the symptoms of PTSD. It is like hurriedly hiding things behind cushions when an unexpected visitor arrives rather than tidying away things to their proper place.

Normal memories are:

- organised
- easy to bring to mind
- easy to describe in words
- remembered as happening in the past
- updated by new information.

Trauma memories are:

- disorganised; they do not have a beginning, middle and end
- fragmented; small pieces of the event might be vivid but other parts might be hazy or missing

- experienced as current; when recalled the event is experienced as happening in the present rather than the past
- not updated; new information about the event or one's reactions does not become incorporated into the memory
- not voluntarily recalled; the trauma memory can pop into one's mind when least expected and can be hard to recall when we want to
- easily triggered; particular reminders of the event, eg noises, smells or images can bring the traumatic event to life again.

Common symptoms

There are many symptoms associated with PTSD; the most common are:

- *Re-experiencing.* This can include distressing nightmares, seeing distressing images in one's head, hallucinations of the event, and 'flashbacks'; these experiences are often so vivid that they are experienced as if they were really happening and can be very intense and frightening.
- *'Flashback'* is the term used for specific vivid and intrusive trauma memories. They can include physical sensations, voices, smells and the experience of fear. Flashbacks are usually triggered by something which is connected to the trauma memory, eg a physical sensation. Nightmares and flashbacks are very similar.
- *Avoidance.* Because re-experiencing can be triggered by reminders of the event it is not surprising that people try to avoid potential triggers. This includes external reminders such as situations or people as well as internal reminders such as thoughts and emotions.
- *Numbing.* It is likely that avoidance can lead to numbing as a way of protecting oneself from feeling emotional pain. This also includes feelings of detachment and dissociation.
- *Dissociation.* This is the feeling of being 'spaced out' or feeling as if things are not real or are happening in a film. It can feel as if you are in a dream or on 'auto-pilot'.
- *Hyper-arousal.* Being very alert to noises, being easily startled and having difficulty falling and staying asleep are all symptoms of hyper-arousal.

These symptoms, particularly flashbacks and dissociation, can feel like psychotic symptoms. Learning to recognise and understand these symptoms as trauma memory reactions can help to make these experiences more manageable and reduce worry that they are signs of relapse.

Treatment for PTSD

If you don't like something change it, if you can't change it change the way you think about it.

Mary Engelbreit

There are several psychological interventions which have been found to be very successful in the treatment of PTSD.

These include:

- Learning new ways of coping with distressing symptoms such as flashbacks, nightmares and dissociation. These include grounding techniques which help you to return to the present moment.
- Identifying and coping with triggers.
- Changing one's thoughts and feelings associated with the event (cognitive re-structuring).
- Giving up unhelpful coping strategies which keep the symptoms going.
- Transferring your memory of the event from the part of the brain which contains trauma memory to the part which contains normal memories. This involves going through the event in detail and helping you to organise and control the memory until it is stored in the usual way.

Not all interventions are appropriate for everyone. Your therapist will discuss your treatment goals with you and together you can draw up a treatment plan.

6 Mood **disturbance** in psychosis

Mood disturbance is a common problem in people with a diagnosis of psychosis.

The perceived role and importance of mood in psychosis has changed over time and continues to cause debate today. Eugen Bleuler, who coined the term 'Schizophrenia' in 1908, proposed that problems of affect were central to schizophrenia and that delusions and hallucinations were merely 'accessory'. A distinction is often drawn between affective psychoses which involve clear mood components, for example schizoaffective disorder, and non-affective psychosis, such as schizophrenia and delusional disorder, which are seen as unrelated to mood disturbance. Karl Jaspers, the German psychiatrist and philosopher, proposed a hierarchical approach to diagnosis in which affective symptoms are 'trumped' by schizophrenia in terms of diagnosis and treatment; his ideas remain influential today.

Thus mood disorders are often subsumed by a diagnosis of psychosis rather than seen as separate co-morbid disorders. In people diagnosed with schizophrenia, mood can often be overlooked if it is not a primary presenting problem. However, many people with psychosis experience depressed mood, elation and/or problematic mood variation.

Mood disturbance presentations

There are several diagnoses in which mood is central.

Schizoaffective disorder is a disorder in which the key features of major depression, mania or mixed episodes occur along with the characteristic symptoms of schizophrenia. Schizoaffective disorder can feature bipolar or depressive mood states. However, psychotic symptoms also occur in the absence of mood disturbance and to receive a diagnosis of schizoaffective disorder the criterion of experiencing psychotic symptoms for at least two weeks during a period of normal mood must be met.

Bipolar disorder, in which the person experiences major depressive as well as manic episodes, is classified as a mood disorder, rather than a psychotic disorder.

However, psychotic symptoms including delusions and hallucinations are also common in bipolar disorder.

Severe depression, in which delusions, hallucinations or 'depressive stupor' co-occur, is sometimes referred to as psychotic depression. Delusions and hallucinations can be mood-congruent or mood-incongruent.

There is a broad range of mood-related problems; sometimes discrete episodes of elation or depression can be identified but just as common are fluctuations in mood or mixed presentations where depression can co-exist with periods of elation. Mood disturbance is best seen as falling on a continuum which can change and fluctuate over time. Within this are many variations in mood which can be problematic. A list of terms and definitions related to mood disturbance is shown in Box 6.1.

Box 6.1 Mood disturbance: definitions

Mania: Mood disturbance characterised by inflated self-esteem, grandiosity, decreased need for sleep, pressure of speech, talkativeness, flight of ideas, racing thoughts, distractibility, increased activity, agitation, excessive involvement in pleasurable activities.

Manic episode: Mania for at least one week.

Hypomania: As for mania but with less severe impact on functioning (mild to moderate mania).

Hypomanic episode: Hypomania for at least four days.

Hyperthymic: Mild elevations in mood.

Depression: Mood disturbance characterised by lasting sad, anxious or empty mood, feelings of hopelessness or pessimism, feelings of guilt, worthlessness or helplessness, loss of interest in pleasurable activities, decreased energy, difficulty concentrating, restlessness, irritability, sleep disturbance, change in appetite, thoughts of death or suicide. Symptoms experienced for at least two weeks.

Dysthymia: Mild reduction in mood.

Cyclothymia: Recurrent episodes of mild mood disturbance which varies between hypomania and dysthymic mood.

Euthymia: Normal harmonious mood.

An interesting and influential study of over 7,000 people looked at the underlying structure of symptoms of depression, mania and psychosis in a general population sample. The survey found that in the general population, seven correlated but separable dimensions of experiences exist that resemble dimensions of psychopathology seen in clinical samples with severe mental illness. These were: core depression, sleep problems, suicidal thoughts, mania, paranoid delusions, first-rank delusions and hallucinations. The substantial correlations between these dimensions in clinical and non-clinical samples may suggest that there is an aetiological overlap between the different dimensions regardless of level of severity and diagnosable disorder (Krabbendam *et al*, 2004).

While having a definitive diagnosis is important for the valid prescribing of medication, the majority of psychological treatments do not rely upon formal diagnosis. The focus is upon presenting problems rather than treatment corresponding to diagnosis; for example, sleep disturbance can occur in both mania and depression.

Psychotic symptoms including delusions and hallucinations can occur in both mania and in depression. The symptoms tend to reflect the extreme mood state at the time. For example, in periods of mania a person might develop grandiose delusions of being all-powerful and invincible. In depression delusions of guilt and worthlessness might arise such as believing one has committed a terrible crime or one's family is doomed.

Prevalence and significance of mood disturbance in psychosis

Depression is very common in the general population; in an American national sample the lifetime prevalence of major depression was estimated to be approximately 17 per cent (Blazer *et al*, 1994). A survey of primary care patients found psychosis proneness to be associated with a greater risk for depression. The authors of the survey suggest that a continuum of vulnerability might exist between affective disorder and non-affective psychosis (Verdoux *et al*, 1999).

A study into the occurrence and persistence of depression during the course of schizophrenia compared depression in schizophrenia with that in schizoaffective and major depressive disorders. Patients with a variety of severe mental illnesses were assessed during hospitalisation and prospectively for depression, psychosis, and post-hospital functioning. It was found that 30 per cent to 40 per cent of patients with schizophrenia had depression at four- and seven-year follow up, including a subgroup of patients who had repeated depression. Depression in schizophrenia was associated with poor overall outcome, work impairment, lower activity, dissatisfaction and suicidal tendencies. Those with schizophrenia and depression had much poorer post-hospital adjustment in terms of employment, rehospitalisation, and psychosis than did the patients with primary major depression. The researchers found that a continuum of vulnerability to depression contributes to the heterogeneity of schizophrenia, with some patients being prone to depression even years after the acute phase (Sands and Harrow, 1999).

People with a diagnosis of schizophrenia were found to have poorer insight compared with those with schizoaffective disorder and psychotic unipolar depression. However, no difference in insight was found with those with bipolar disorder (Pini *et al*, 2001).

Lake (2008) proposes that severe disorders of mood are also disorders of thought. He argues that as selective attention becomes defective in mania, tangential stimuli are processed without prioritisation. This causes distractibility and accounts for the signs and symptoms of psychotic thinking. He points out that no symptoms of thought disorder and speech such as tangentiality, derailment, thought blocking and echolalia are specific for schizophrenia and are more likely to be explained by the core manic symptom of distractibility.

Assessment of mood disturbance

Mood Disorders Questionnaire (MDQ) (Hirschfeld *et al*, 2000)

This questionnaire was developed as a brief self-report screening instrument for bipolar spectrum disorders. Clients answer 'yes' or 'no' to a series of 13 statements indicative of unusual mood-dependent symptoms and behaviours such as feeling much more self-confident; therefore it is useful in the assessment of the impact and nature of the clients' difficulties. Functional impairment is also gauged on a four-point scale.

Internal States Scale (ISS) (Bauer *et al*, 1991)

This is a self-report instrument for the simultaneous assessment of severity of manic and depressive symptoms. It consists of four empirically derived subscales: Activation, Well-Being, Perceived Conflict, and the Depression Index. It is very useful for monitoring current mood and therefore, if completed regularly, can provide information on fluctuations or stabilisation during treatment.

Hypomania Interpretations Questionnaire (HIQ) (Jones *et al*, 2006)

This 10-item questionnaire was designed to assess positive self-dispositional appraisals for hypomania-relevant experiences. It has two subscales which measure positive self-dispositional appraisals (HIQ-H) and normalising appraisals (HIQ-NE). Thus it highlights the presence of unhelpful cognitive styles which can then be addressed in treatment. It is a reliable and valid measure for the assessment of positive self-dispositional appraisals that seem to be linked to both hypomanic personality and bipolar disorder.

The relevance of such appraisals for symptom exacerbation and potential relapse can be investigated during CBT (*see* treatment section).

Social Rhythm Metric (SRM) (Monk *et al*, 1990)

This is an instrument designed to quantify an individual's daily social rhythms. Social rhythms are important both as a way of structuring the day cognitively and as time cues that drive the biological clock (circadian system). The SRM lists activities which can be noted as regular; ie, engaged in three or more times per week. The frequency of each regular activity can be recorded which gives a measure of stability. This is useful as a monitor of stability and of change pre- and post-treatment.

Calgary Depression Scale (CDS) (Addington *et al*, 1993)

A widely used tool specifically developed for the assessment of the level of depression in schizophrenia. It has been evaluated in both relapsed and remitted clients and appears sensitive to change. In a review of depression scales in schizophrenia the Calgary was considered to be a well-documented and validated tool with an unidimensional structure, a good internal consistency, a high inter-rater reliability and a good external validity and specificity (Reine *et al*, 1998). It is a nine-item clinician-rated semi-structured interview covering aspects such as suicidal ideation, hopelessness and self-deprecation. Scores are allocated on a basis of severity: absent, mild, medium or severe on a four-point scale, considering the previous two weeks. A score above 6 has an 82 per cent specificity and an 85 per cent sensitivity for predicting the presence of a major depressive episode. The CDS is presented in the Appendix (*see* p. 148). (*See also* Chapter 2 'Negative symptoms'.)

Hypomanic Attitudes and Positive Predictions Inventory (HAPPI) (Mansell, 2006)

This self-report inventory assesses extreme appraisals of internal states. The scale identifies the cognitions that characterise bipolar affective disorder and that may influence the development of mania or hypomania. Six factors representing distinct categories of beliefs about internal states are measured: social self-criticism, increasing activation to avoid failure, success activation and triumph over fear, loss of control, goal appraisals for creating and success, and regaining autonomy (Dodd *et al*, 2011a). The HAPPI can be used as a tool in CBT to identify problematic beliefs and to guide formulation (Dodd *et al*, 2011b). A short form is available.

Working model of mood disturbance

The model is based upon the vulnerability-stress model of schizophrenia (Nuechterlein and Dawson, 1984) modified for bipolar disorder (Lam *et al*, 1999). It proposes that life events and other stressors raise the risk of an episode in those with increased vulnerability to mood disturbance. In particular, sensitivity of the circadian system, which maintains the daily physiological rhythms, is likely to

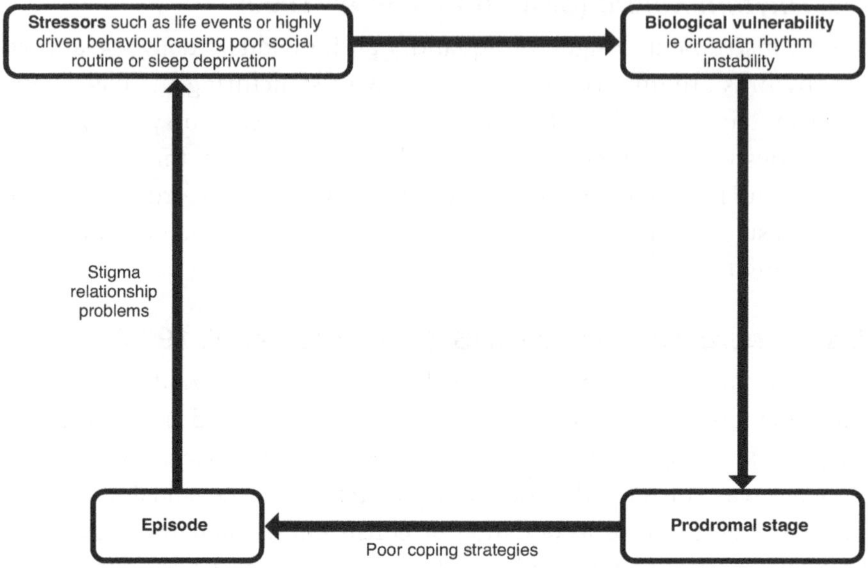

FIGURE 6.1 Working model of mood disturbance

Reproduced with kind permission from Jones S (2004) 'Psychotherapy of bipolar disorder: a review', *Journal of Affective Disorders*, 80, pp101–14. Elsevier.

be a central vulnerability factor (Goodwin and Jamison, 1990). Thus stressors cause disruption to the sleep pattern or daily routine. Prodromal changes such as excessive energy or agitation follow. The person's responses to these changes can exacerbate symptoms; those with poor or ineffective coping strategies being more likely to experience an episode. Consequences of the episode, such as relationship problems, can lead to further stress and so continue the cycle.

CASE VIGNETTE: DESMOND

Desmond is a 33-year-old man who was born in London of Kenyan parentage. He was the eldest of nine children, two of whom died in infancy. Desmond did well at school and was an outgoing and sociable boy. He excelled at sport and played for his county cricket team. His mother had several admissions to psychiatric hospital during his childhood; during her absences his father employed a nanny. Desmond left school at 16 having attained good grades in all subjects. He completed a course in business studies before starting his own business importing African artefacts which he sold via the internet.

Desmond married an English woman who worked as an interior designer. Shortly after the birth of their child, Desmond began to behave in an erratic way. He exercised excessively, worked increasingly long hours and stayed up at night to buy goods and to frequent internet 'chat-rooms' on his laptop. He amassed considerable credit-card debts buying generous gifts for his large family and for friends. He ordered takeaway meals to be delivered in the early hours of the morning and refused to eat with his wife and child. He questioned whether he was the father of the baby whom he described as 'too white'. Desmond was admitted to hospital after attempting to strangle his wife and telling police officers that she had been 'replaced'. He believed that he was a multi-millionaire who ran a successful company employing 100 people. He was diagnosed with schizoaffective disorder.

Formulation for Desmond

Using the working model, Desmond and his therapist drew up a formulation in order to help to understand his manic episode (*see* Figure 6.2). Desmond had experienced a number of stressors immediately prior to this episode: he and his wife had moved into their first house and taken on a large mortgage. Their child was born three months later and due to medical complications his wife and baby remained in hospital for several weeks.

During this period Desmond started to work increasingly long hours; he described feeling under pressure to provide for his family and he was worried that his baby would die. He had experienced the loss of his 2-year-old brother when he was 5 and his baby sister when he was aged 8. These bereavements were reactivated and he became preoccupied with thoughts of loss. His visits to the hospital decreased as he found them too distressing. He was unable to sleep and spent increasing time on the internet. He bought weights and a rowing machine and exercised excessively. As he worked from home, he had limited social contact and only communicated with family and friends via the internet.

Desmond's family history revealed a likely biological predisposition: his mother, brother and sister all had contact with mental health services; his brother committed suicide in a psychiatric hospital at age 24 years. Although this appears to have been Desmond's first psychotic experience, he described previous periods of elation and occasional low mood from age 16 years. These seemed to have occurred in response to life changes such as leaving school, the death of his brother, his marriage and a failed business partnership.

The prodromal phase was identified as having four components: decreased sleep, excessive energy, impulsivity in decision making and thoughts that the baby was not his own. He made uncharacteristic rash decisions such as purchasing goods in large quantities before testing the market.

His attempts to cope with the pressures only served to compound his excessive behaviours. He slept less, worked longer hours, spent money buying expensive gifts and withdrew entirely from social contact. He stopped visiting his wife and baby. When they returned home he experienced his wife as 'cold and distant' and he started to believe that not only was the child not his but that his wife was an imposter. It is possible that early memories of his mother literally being replaced by a series of nannies might have played a part in the formation of this delusional belief. He also believed that his business decisions had made him very wealthy and that his 'replacement' wife wanted his money; this culminated on an attack on his wife who finally left him.

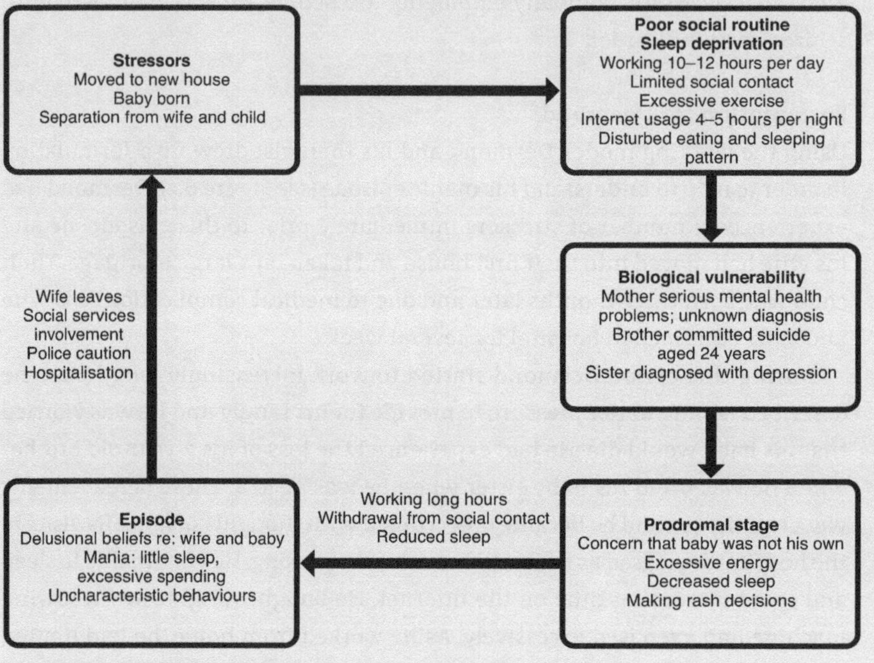

FIGURE 6.2 Working model case example: Desmond

Treatment of mood disturbance

The most appropriate treatment for mood disturbance will be informed by the presenting problems and the client formulation. CBT for depression is a well-established and effective treatment. The process and techniques have been described in key texts by Beck and others (Beck, 1976). This section will focus upon elevated and fluctuating mood. This treatment approach draws on the work of Steven Jones and colleagues (eg Jones, 2004; Lam *et al*, 1999). A typical treatment plan is shown in Box 6.2.

Box 6.2 Treatment plan for client with mood disturbance

1. Exploration of presenting problems, engagement and history taking including detailed history of all episodes. Formulation using working model.
2. Formal assessment using, for example, MDQ, HQ, ISS, SRM.
3. Agree and decide on format of regular mood monitoring.
4. Goal setting and barriers to change; focus on resistance to inhibiting high mood.
5. Establish links between events, mood and behaviour.
6. Stabilise sleep and activity patterns.
7. Deal with positive interpretations and dysfunctional assumptions.
8. Identify prodromes.
9. Develop coping strategies, eg delaying tactics, enhancing self-management.
10. Staying well planning.

Mood monitoring

Monitoring of mood is a simple but vital component of treatment. It should begin early in therapy and continue throughout. It is important for three main reasons: 1) it enables the client to cultivate familiarity with and awareness of their own mood states; 2) it encourages recognition of what is 'normal' mood; 3) it enhances

TABLE 6.1 Mood monitoring chart

Mood rating: –10 to +10
Week starting (date): ______________________

	Mon	Tues	Weds	Thurs	Fri	Sat	Sun
6–8 am							
8–10 am							
10–12 am							
12–2 pm							
2–4 pm							
4–6 pm							
6–8 pm							
8–10 pm							
10–12 pm							
12–2 am							
2–4 am							
4–6 am							

detection of early warning signs which is important in the identification of prodromes. A sample mood rating sheet is shown in Table 6.1 this chart also allows monitoring during the night if the person has sleep disturbance.

Following a period of monitoring, agreement of what constitutes normal mood for the client can be decided. This is likely to range, for example, between –5 and +5; anything beyond this range can then be used to 'flag up' problematic mood.

NB: Some clients might prefer to monitor their mood electronically.

Goal setting and barriers to change

Unlike other mental health problems, high mood is often not presented as problematic by the client; those with mood elevation frequently enjoy the experience and do not seek help to change. People frequently describe their high moods as a positive experience in which they feel more alive, creative and productive. Engagement and goal setting with such clients therefore requires careful consideration of the reasons for working towards mood stability rather than allowing high mood to persist. Client information sheet 6.1 describes reasons to reduce elevated mood.

Discussions about tackling elevated mood can be assisted by reviewing the client's history for any notable sequelae to or consequences of high mood. It can be helpful to ask the client to bring to mind anything which they generally regret doing when they were high and to explore any specific instances, eg of spending, drinking, drug taking, arguments, and inappropriate behaviour. They might also consider asking friends or relatives how they experience the person during periods of elevated mood: do they find them fun and exciting or exhausting and inaccessible?

Goal setting must, of course, be collaborative and personally meaningful. Relevant goals might include wider life goals which are not necessarily typical CBT targets – for example, *see* Desmond's goals. These can usually be broken down into CBT goals by exploring what steps might need to precede the ultimate goal.

Example goals: Desmond

1. Get back with my wife.
2. Sort out my finances and don't spend any money on unnecessary things.
3. Stick to a regular routine.
4. Stop using chat rooms.
5. Get my business back on track.

CLIENT INFORMATION SHEET 6.1 – I'M HAPPY THIS WAY: 10 REASONS TO REDUCE ELEVATED MOOD

We may outrun by violent swiftness . . . and lose by over-running.

William Shakespeare, *Henry VIII*

1. The way you perceive yourself can be very different from the way others experience you: talkative and eloquent versus loud and verbose, cheerful and jocular versus inappropriate and annoying, gregarious versus over the top.
2. While reduced need for sleep might seem appealing it can lead to inattention, carelessness and reduced efficiency as well as physical health problems, eg making you more susceptible to illness.
3. Just as low mood can make decision making difficult and lead to procrastination, high mood can lead to making impulsive and rash decisions which one later regrets.
4. Feeling uninhibited and carefree is a small step away from being disinhibited and reckless, which can lead to risk taking in sexual behaviour, driving, drinking and other potentially dangerous activities.
5. High mood can impair judgement: one is more likely to be exploited or taken advantage of when feeling high. Similarly, a business deal or new venture might seem more inviting if one does not see the potential drawbacks.
6. Confidence and optimism are helpful when realistic; being over-confident and over-optimistic can lead to a fall.
7. Increased productivity is not usually matched by increased quality.
8. Irresponsibility in spending money is very commonly related to increases, as well as decreases, in mood. Large purchases such as a new car require careful and rational thought.
9. Excess in anything, even things which are good for you such as exercise, can lead to problems if they are not regulated.
10. Relationships, work and social activities thrive on stability. Attaining a stable elevated mood is not possible – in reality 'highs' are generally unstable and can lead to depression.

Be moderate in order to taste the joys of life in abundance.

Epicurus

Establishing links between events, mood and behaviour

Enabling the client to see links between events and their changes in mood and behaviour is valuable in a number of ways. Clients often describe their moods as changing 'out of the blue' or for 'no apparent reason' – however, this is rarely the case. While mood changes can appear to arise spontaneously this is usually due to lack of awareness of one's sensitivity to events. Becoming more in touch with one's thoughts, feelings and behaviours in relation to events is a core ability which enhances progress in therapy. Knowledge of what is likely to trigger mood changes helps clients to make sense of them and to feel less at the mercy of apparently spontaneous changes. Coping strategies can then be developed in order to reduce the impact of such events and thereby reduce mood and behavioural reactions. Attributing mood and behaviour changes to events rather than to internal or biological causes also helps to normalise them and to reduce worry over apparently unpredictable mood swings.

There are two main methods which can be used in establishing the link between events, mood and behaviour. First, construct a *timeline* of key events in the person's life. This can be expanded by adding episodes of high and/or low mood and episodes of psychosis. The timeline is a concise and straightforward way to review one's personal history and to pinpoint significant events in order to demonstrate how such events influence mood and behaviour. Invite the client to recall their earliest experience of problematic mood or behaviour and establish their age and any life events at this time; repeat for each further episode. An example timeline is shown in Box 6.3.

Box 6.3 Example timeline to show event-mood-behaviour link

Age 16: Left school	Hypomania, sleep disturbance
Age 21: Death of brother	Depressed mood, not eating
Age 23: Left home	Hypomania, alcohol use
Age 26: Marriage	Hypomania, sleep disturbance
Age 27: Failed business partnership	Depression, crying and irritability
Age 28: Financial problems	Low mood, appetite disturbance
Age 33: New house, baby, illness	Mania and psychotic episode

Second, having established the link between major events and mood or behaviour, invite the client to investigate the current relationship between events and their mood fluctuations. This can be accomplished by keeping a weekly events record in conjunction with their mood monitoring, which can help to identify what might have triggered poor sleep or low mood. Mapping out events and mood or behaviour in this way can show the link in action and provide current material to review in session. Problem solving is often suggested by specific event-mood links; if, for example, low mood is linked to arguments with a partner, then couple counselling might be indicated. An example event/activity record is shown in Table 6.2.

TABLE 6.2 Event/activity record

Time	Monday	Tuesday	Wednesday	Thursday	Friday	Saturday	Sunday
8–9 am	Breakfast						
9–10 am	TV						
10–11 am	TV						
11–12 am	Shops						
12–1 pm	Lunch						
1–2 pm	Café with Jill						
2–3 pm	Walked in park						
3–4 pm	Cleaned flat						
4–5 pm	TV						
5–6 pm	Made dinner						
6–7 pm	Dinner						
7–8 pm	Argument with John						
8–9 pm	Bath						
9–10 pm	Read in bed						
10–11 pm	Asleep						

Stabilising sleep and activity patterns

Too much or too little sleep can be detrimental to physical and mental health. Changes to the 24-hour pattern of sleep and wakefulness, the circadian rhythm, are common in mood disturbance. Stabilising sleep and activity can help to reduce the impact of such changes.

Circadian activity can be monitored by wearing a small device on the wrist, known as an actiwatch. This detects and logs movement intensity and duration. Data is stored on the watch and can be downloaded to a computer for analysis. Thus general physical activity can be gauged and activity plots compared over time to monitor changes and response to treatment. If this device is not available, simple sleep charts can be kept by the client to document hours of sleep in each 24-hour period.

Interventions to stabilise sleep patterns generally follow three steps:

1. Establish what a 'normal' period of sleep is for the client. Remember that this might not be what is desirable, particularly if they prefer hypomania; sleep

is not dispensable! People typically function most effectively with 8 hours of sleep, plus or minus one hour, in each 24-hour period.

2. Once this is agreed as a target, sleep can be scheduled into their routine, eg from 11 pm to 7 am.
3. Draw up a plan to assist with insomnia and to develop a sleep pattern.

An example insomnia action plan is presented in Box 6.4.

Box 6.4 Tackling insomnia action plan

- Enjoy a 'winding down' hour before going to bed to prepare the body and mind for sleep. This might include: dimming the lights, having a warm bath, reading a book, listening to soft music.
- Go to bed only when you start to feel sleepy. This is preferable to lying in bed wide awake (even if you have to stay up late initially).
- Do not watch TV, eat, drink or read in bed.
- If you have not fallen asleep within 20 minutes, get up and go into another room; do something to help induce sleep, eg read a book, listen to quiet, slow music.
- Return to bed when feeling sleepy.
- If not asleep after 20 minutes repeat as above; this is hard but better than lying awake in bed.
- Set the alarm and get up at the target time even if you are tired and did not sleep very much.
- Do not sleep during the day.

The social rhythm metric (SRM) can be very helpful in gauging regular activities and disruptions to routine. It provides a list of activities such as meal times, bed time and rising times. These activities can be regarded as regular if they occur at least three times per week within 45 minutes of the habitual time for that event. For each regular activity, the client rates how frequently that activity occurs and thus gives a measure of stability. Completing the SRM at the start and end of therapy also provides a measure of treatment change.

Addressing positive interpretations and dysfunctional assumptions

Dysfunctional assumptions and interpretations about symptoms can have implications for symptom exacerbation and potential relapse. Interpretations of hypomanic symptoms, such as racing thoughts, might be attributed internally, eg 'I'm having lots of great ideas', or externally 'There is too much to do at the moment'. *The Hypomanic Interpretations Questionnaire* (HIQ) lists such symptoms and provides two alternative explanations: one internal and one external. The HIQ is very helpful in highlighting assumptions about the person's 'true self' which can be a focus for CBT. The aim is to increase external interpretations which will, in turn, enhance motivation to act to reduce the symptoms and their impact.

If a person interprets their increased impulsivity as their being efficient and decisive they are not likely to take steps to reduce this. However, if they view it as indicating that they have too many external demands they are more likely to take action to reduce those demands to prevent rash decisions.

Reviews of beliefs, behaviour and outcomes during mood elevations provide an impartial source of evidence for those who hold positive interpretations of symptoms (*see* Box 6.5 Addressing assumptions: Desmond)

Behavioural experiments are another good way of helping the client to discover whether or not their assumptions are accurate.

Box 6.5 Addressing assumptions: Desmond

Review of outcomes

Desmond continued to hold the belief that he made good business decisions when he was 'high'.

He agreed to conduct a review in order to investigate this assumption.

Desmond compared stock purchase to sales figures for the two months prior to his elevated mood and in the subsequent two months.

He was very surprised to find that, although he had been working much longer hours during the period when he was 'high', he had had better sales figures for the first two months. In addition, he had substantially over-bought stock which had not sold in the second period. The review helped him to understand that recognising when he was high and putting in place safeguards against impulsive decisions would be of benefit to him and his business.

Identifying prodromes

Once the client has a good understanding of their mood, thoughts and behaviour and they are able to link events and mood, the prodrome can be examined in more detail. Extreme mood changes do not occur spontaneously or without warning – usually the early signs are not noticed or are ignored. The build-up in quantity, frequency and severity of signs and symptoms can be detected and acted upon. Identification of prodromal signs is vital so that action can be taken to try to avert extreme mood developing or to reduce the effects of mood disturbance while the person still retains insight. The construction of a prodromal 'signature' is detailed in Box 6.6. While many signs will be idiosyncratic, a number of common signs are likely to occur. Typical signs and symptoms can be presented on pre-prepared cards to help to identify all applicable signs and these can be modified to fit the client's experience. Common signs are listed in Box 6.7. An example prodromal signature is shown in Box 6.8.

NB: This 'card sort' technique can be used to identify early signs in any disorder which has a prodromal period, such as psychosis and depression.

Box 6.6 Constructing a prodromal signature for mania

- Provide a set of cards each containing one common prodromal sign for mania.
- Ask the client to go through the cards, separating them into two piles in order to identify signs which have preceded previous episodes of mania and discarding any which are not relevant.
- Add any additional idiosyncratic signs or symptoms on separate index cards.
- Ask the client to sort the cards into three piles to signify the stages of the prodrome:
  - Green/Early (eg 5+ days prior to episode)
  - Amber/Mid (eg 2–4 days prior)
  - Red/Late (eg 24 hours prior)
- Remember that time scales will vary for each client.
- Specify which of these signs have preceded one or more previous episodes.

Box 6.7 Common prodromal signs for mania

- Full of energy
- Suicidal thoughts
- Over-activity
- Feeling superior to others
- Feeling reckless
- Taking on too much
- Not needing much sleep or being unable to sleep
- Feeling creative
- Feeling different from others
- Irritability
- Can't be bothered do to normal tasks
- Difficulty concentrating
- Acting in an uninhibited way
- Being excitable

- Increased interest in sex
- Racing thoughts
- Feeling religious or spiritual
- Being extravagant
- Bizarre or unusual thoughts
- Feeling very self-confident
- Change in appetite
- Talkative
- More outgoing and gregarious
- Feeling alert
- Heightened senses
- Cheerful and full of fun
- Very optimistic
- Carefree
- Feeling of physical fitness

Box 6.8 Example prodromal signature

Green signs/ symptoms (5+ days prior)	Amber signs/ symptoms (2–4 days prior)	Red signs/symptoms (24 hours prior)
Feeling more self-confident	Difficulty focusing	Very full of energy
Staying up later	Full of ideas and plans	Stop going to work; busy with new projects
More talkative	Anxious or worrying	Talking rapidly and at length
Feeling energetic	Jogging, gym, cycling 2–4 hours a day	Racing thoughts
Walk to work	Talking on phone for hours	Bizarre thoughts
Cycle in evenings	Difficulty sleeping 4–5 hours per night	Very little sleep (1–2 hours)
Cheerful and carefree		Excitable
		Spending money on things I don't need

Coping strategies

As illustrated by the working model, poor or ineffective responses to prodromal signs are central to the likelihood of progression to an episode. Therefore successful coping strategies are a vital component to the management of mood disturbance. There are a number of techniques for generating coping strategies:

1. Match strategies to each prodromal sign

Coping strategies can be developed for each of the prodromal signs; there are therefore many ways to help the person to stabilise their own mood. Examples include: reduce caffeine, go to bed at a regular time, develop a routine, have regular meal times, timetable activity, challenge thoughts. Making small changes to retain control can be very successful.

2. Cue cards

The client will often have good ideas about how to manage their own behaviour when low or high. The ability or motivation to carry out such ideas will, of course, be compromised when actually experiencing the mood disturbance. Therefore it can be helpful to examine the client's ideas in detail when they are in a stable mood state and to assist them to formalise an agreement with themself to avoid risk taking and impulsivity when their mood changes. At such times it is easy to dismiss ideas as 'just what my therapist says', so using the client's own words and ideas is likely to be more successful.

Such 'wise self' advice can be written on cards which can be kept in the most appropriate place – wallet, car, fridge door – to provide a reminder from themself to themself. Examples include:

- 'Don't buy anything over £50 today.'
- 'Make no big decisions for 48 hours.'
- 'If you think it's a brilliant idea it probably isn't!'

3. Game-show strategy

This strategy is based on a popular television game show in which the contestant has three 'life lines' to help them. Each 'life line' should be tailored to the client and made as specific as possible.

1. 'Ask the audience'. This might be as simple as having the client ask themself, 'What would most people do or say in this situation?' Mini-surveys can also be conducted in which the client asks a small number of people what they would do.
2. '50:50'. This requires the client to take away the most dramatic or extreme response and leave a more tempered or reversible solution.
3. 'Phone a friend'. Identify one or two people whom the client could contact when at risk of making rash decisions or when they need good advice.

Identification of such a person should include exploration of why that person is suitable, eg choose a person who is able to provide independent expert advice rather than a friend who always agrees with them.

Clients will generally have developed their own coping strategies and a variety of strategies are often used. There is no single recommended strategy or set of strategies. The most important element is what works for the individual. Common strategies are list in Box 6.9.

Box 6.9 Mood-related coping strategies

Mood management and self-awareness

- Noticing warning signs and using coping strategies
- Gaining a better understanding of mood swings
- Understanding the types of thing that might be triggers for oneself
- Acceptance of normal energy levels
- Using self-help resources

Psychological

- Learning to be more empathic and forgiving of oneself
- Learning to recognise when the way we are thinking may be unhelpful or biased
- Moderating success and perfectionism

Interpersonal

- Developing and maintaining supportive relationships
- Learning to assert one's own needs
- Learning to grow from, rather than feel crushed by criticism, rejection or disagreement
- Choosing with whom, and when, to talk about bipolar disorder
- Sharing a relapse plan with significant others

Physical wellness

- Eating healthily and regularly
- Not relying on alcohol, tobacco or substances
- Exercise
- Relaxation

Identity

- Having meaning and purpose
- Self-awareness and acceptance

- Not seeing bipolar as the defining feature of one's identity
- Self-appreciation – recognising one's strengths as well as one's difficulties

Support from services
- Making informed decisions about medication
- Access to psychological therapies
- Supportive relationships with services
- Being involved in decisions about one's care and treatments

Spirituality and faith
- Having faith in a deity (or deities)
- Connection with one's spirituality
- Being at one with nature
- Using meditation, yoga or visualisation

Self-care
- Having 'me' time
- Building up lifestyle fundamentals (eg lower stress, daily routine, good sleep)
- Being involved in personally meaningful activities (such as work, further learning or creativity)
- Taking time out to relax
- The opportunity to stimulate senses (eg massage or aromatherapy)
- Taking responsibility for one's actions
- Being involved in care planning decisions

Hope and optimism
- Experiencing success
- Taking control
- Working towards personally meaningful goals
- Self-belief that one can cope and manage

Risk and responsibility
- Having the freedom to make choices and mistakes
- Having support and advice regarding financial risks and difficulties

From: British Psychological Society (2010) *Understanding Bipolar Disorder*, reproduced with kind permission of BPS.

Staying-well plans

Staying-well plans are a summary of the main ideas, concepts and information that the person has found useful during the course of therapy. They are written by the client in their own words with encouragement and help as needed. Some people might choose to write a straightforward list, while others might create a poster or collage. The plan could be carried in a wallet, as a memo in a mobile phone, or put in a diary or on the wall. The staying-well plan complements the prodrome information. An example staying-well plan is shown in Box 6.10.

RECOMMENDED READING:

The British Psychological Society (2010) *Understanding Bipolar Disorder, Why Some People Experience Extreme Mood States and What Can Help*, Division of Clinical Psychology, BPS.

Lam D, Jones S, Hayward P & Bright J (1999) *Cognitive Therapy for Bipolar Disorders: A Therapist's Guide to Concepts, Methods and Practice*, Wiley, Chichester.

Box 6.10 Example staying-well plan

1. I am not alone with this problem; hundreds of people have mood changes and manage OK.
2. Don't forget that other people are happy to help; ask Mum, Dave and Jo when I need help or advice.
3. Mania seems like fun but can get me into stupid situations; I will look after myself and caring for myself means trying to 'put the brakes on', not getting carried away and not allowing my mood to just escalate.
4. Watch those prodromes!
5. Try to keep to my bed times and get enough sleep.
6. Thoughts are just thoughts: I don't have to take them as true.
7. Suicidal thoughts don't stay long so ignore them don't take them seriously.
8. Watch my activity levels and keep to my weekly planner.
9. I don't have to be liked by everyone to be happy.
10. 'Me time' is more important than getting everything done.
11. Breathe!
12. Meditate.

CLIENT INFORMATION SHEET 6.2 – UNDERSTANDING MOOD DISTURBANCE

We all experience changes in our moods and emotions; sometimes these are obvious (crying or sadness) and sometimes they are more subtle (irritation or annoyance). Usually our moods change in response to a situation or event and the way we think about it. Sometimes these changes are fast and short-lived, eg sadness at seeing starving children on the television news followed by joy and laughter at a comedy show. However, mood changes can become problematic when they are more extreme, last a long time and start to interfere with our daily lives.

You might have been diagnosed with a mood disorder such as depression or mania as well as psychosis, because often the two occur together. Often a diagnosis of 'schizoaffective disorder' is made when the key features of either major depression, mania or a mixed episode occur with the characteristic symptoms of schizophrenia.

Common symptoms in mood disturbance

Mood disturbance can affect people in a number of ways including changes in:

- sleep
- appetite
- communication
- thinking
- activity levels
- energy levels
- concentration
- emotions.

Each of these can increase or decrease; talking too much or not at all, being hyperactive or unable to get out of bed, feeling anxious and restless or empty and numb.

What causes mood disturbance?

People who experience strong mood fluctuations often have a biological predisposition; perhaps other people in your family also have or had mental health problems. Mood change is usually triggered by life events or other stressful situations including putting too much pressure on yourself. The situation can be aggravated by lifestyle imbalance such as not getting enough sleep, doing too much, not having a routine. If early changes are not noticed or ignored they can worsen. Sometimes attempts to cope by taking drugs or alcohol make things even worse.

Can it be treated?

The good news is that there are a number of successful treatment strategies for controlling mood disturbance. These involve looking closely at your thoughts, feelings and behaviour in relation to events or situations and understanding how and why your mood fluctuates. This is known as CBT – Cognitive Behavioural Therapy – and treatment includes:

- understanding the links between events, mood and behaviour
- stabilising sleep patterns
- creating a balanced lifestyle including healthy levels of activity
- looking at thoughts and beliefs which influence mood
- identifying early signs of mood change
- developing coping strategies
- examining ways of staying well.

By looking in detail at past and current episodes of mood disturbance it is possible to learn how to identify early changes and to reduce their impact and manage them more effectively.

Smooth seas do not make skilful sailors

African proverb

Appendix

Dissociative Experiences Scale II (DESII)

Reproduced with permission

This questionnaire consists of 28 questions about experiences that you may have in your daily life. We are interested in how often you have these experiences. It is important, however, that your answers show how often these experiences happen to you when you are not under the influence of alcohol or drugs. To answer the question, *please determine to what degree the experience described in the question applies to you and mark the line with a vertical slash at the appropriate place*, as shown in the example below.

Example:

0 |————————————/————————————| 100%

1. Some people have the experience of driving a car and suddenly realising that they don't remember what happened during all or part of the trip. Mark the line to show what percentage of the time this happens to you.

   0 |————————————————————————| 100%

2. Some people find that sometimes they are listening to someone talk and they suddenly realise that they did not hear part or all of what was just said. Mark the line to show what percentage of the time this happens to you.

   0 |————————————————————————| 100%

3. Some people have the experience of finding themselves in a place and having no idea how they got there. Mark the line to show what percentage of the time this happens to you.

   0 |————————————————————————| 100%

4. Some people have the experience of finding themselves dressed in clothes that they don't remember putting on. Mark the line to show what percentage of the time this happens to you.

   0 |———————————————| 100%

5. Some people have the experience of finding new things among their belongings that they do not remember buying. Mark the line to show what percentage of the time this happens to you.

   0 |———————————————| 100%

6. Some people sometimes find that they are approached by people that they do not know who call them by another name or insist that they have met them before. Mark the line to show what percentage of the time this happens to you.

   0 |———————————————| 100%

7. Some people sometimes have the experience of feeling as though they are standing next to themselves as if they were looking at another person. Mark the line to show what percentage of the time this happens to you.

   0 |———————————————| 100%

8. Some people are told that they sometimes do not recognise friends or family members. Mark the line to show what percentage of the time this happens to you.

   0 |———————————————| 100%

9. Some people find that they have no memory for some important events in their lives (for example a wedding or graduation). Mark the line to show what percentage of the important events in your life you have no memory for.

   0 |———————————————| 100%

10. Some people have the experience of being accused of lying when they do not think that they have lied. Mark the line to show what percentage of the time this happens to you.

    0 |———————————————| 100%

11. Some people have the experience of looking in the mirror and not recognising themselves. Mark the line to show what percentage of the time this happens to you.

    0 |———————————————| 100%

12. Some people sometimes have the experience of feeling that other people, objects, and the world around them are not real. Mark the line to show what percentage of the time this happens to you.

    0 |————————————————————| 100%

13. Some people sometimes have the experience of feeling that their body does not seem to belong to them. Mark the line to show what percentage of the time this happens to you.

    0 |————————————————————| 100%

14. Some people have the experience of sometimes remembering a past event so vividly that they feel as if they were reliving that event. Mark the line to show what percentage of the time this happens to you.

    0 |————————————————————| 100%

15. Some people have the experience of not being sure whether things that they remember happening really did happen or whether they just dreamed them. Mark the line to show what percentage of the time this happens to you.

    0 |————————————————————| 100%

16. Some people have the experience of being in a familiar place but finding it strange and unfamiliar. Mark the line to show what percentage of the time this happens to you.

    0 |————————————————————| 100%

17. Some people find that when they are watching television or a movie they become so absorbed in the story that they are unaware of other events happening around them. Mark the line to show what percentage of the time this happens to you.

    0 |————————————————————| 100%

18. Some people sometimes find that they become so involved in a fantasy or daydream that it feels as though it were really happening to them. Mark the line to show what percentage of the time this happens to you.

    0 |————————————————————| 100%

19. Some people find that they sometimes are able to ignore pain. Mark the line to show what percentage of the time this happens to you.

    0 |————————————————————| 100%

20. Some people find that they sometimes sit staring off into space, thinking of nothing, and are not aware of the passage of time. Mark the line to show what percentage of the time this happens to you.

0 |——————————————————| 100%

21. Some people sometimes find that when they are alone they talk out loud to themselves. Mark the line to show what percentage of the time this happens to you.

0 |——————————————————| 100%

22. Some people find that in one situation they may act so differently compared with another situation that they feel almost as if they were two different people. Mark the line to show what percentage of the time this happens to you.

0 |——————————————————| 100%

23. Some people sometimes find that in certain situations they are able to do things with amazing ease and spontaneity that would usually be difficult for them (for example sports, work, social situations etc). Mark the line to show what percentage of the time this happens to you.

0 |——————————————————| 100%

24. Some people sometimes find that they cannot remember whether they have done something or have just thought about doing that thing (mailing a letter). Mark the line to show what percentage of the time this happens to you.

0 |——————————————————| 100%

25. Some people find that they have done things that they do not remember doing. Mark the line to show what percentage of the time this happens to you.

0 |——————————————————| 100%

26. Some people sometimes find writings, drawings, or notes among their belongings that they must have done but cannot remember doing. Mark the line to show what percentage of the time this happens to you.

0 |——————————————————| 100%

27. Some people sometimes find that they hear voices inside their head that tell them to do things or comment on things that they are doing. Mark the line to show what percentage of the time this happens to you.

0 |——————————————————| 100%

28. Some people sometimes feel as if they are looking at the world through a fog so that people and objects appear far away or unclear. Mark the line to show what percentage of the time this happens to you.

0 |————————————————————| 100%

Depression Anxiety Stress Scale (DASS 42)

Reproduced with permission

Full information on this scale can be found at: www.psy.unsw.edu.au/dass/

DASS

Name: Date:

Please read each statement and circle a number 0, 1, 2 or 3 which indicates how much the statement applied to you ***over the past week***. There are no right or wrong answers. Do not spend too much time on any statement.

The rating scale is as follows:

0 Did not apply to me at all
1 Applied to me to some degree, or some of the time
2 Applied to me to a considerable degree, or a good part of time
3 Applied to me very much, or most of the time

1	I found myself getting upset by quite trivial things	0	1	2	3
2	I was aware of dryness of my mouth	0	1	2	3
3	I couldn't seem to experience any positive feeling at all	0	1	2	3
4	I experienced breathing difficulty (eg excessively rapid breathing, breathlessness in the absence of physical exertion)	0	1	2	3
5	I just couldn't seem to get going	0	1	2	3
6	I tended to over-react to situations	0	1	2	3
7	I had a feeling of shakiness (eg legs going to give way)	0	1	2	3
8	I found it difficult to relax	0	1	2	3
9	I found myself in situations that made me so anxious I was most relieved when they ended	0	1	2	3
10	I felt that I had nothing to look forward to	0	1	2	3
11	I found myself getting upset rather easily	0	1	2	3
12	I felt that I was using a lot of nervous energy	0	1	2	3
13	I felt sad and depressed	0	1	2	3
14	I found myself getting impatient when I was delayed in any way (eg lifts, traffic lights, being kept waiting)	0	1	2	3
15	I had a feeling of faintness	0	1	2	3
16	I felt that I had lost interest in just about everything	0	1	2	3
17	I felt I wasn't worth much as a person	0	1	2	3
18	I felt that I was rather touchy	0	1	2	3
19	I perspired noticeably (eg hands sweaty) in the absence of high temperatures or physical exertion	0	1	2	3
20	I felt scared without any good reason	0	1	2	3

DASS

Name: Date:

21	I felt that life wasn't worthwhile	0	1	2	3
22	I found it hard to wind down	0	1	2	3
23	I had difficulty in swallowing	0	1	2	3
24	I couldn't seem to get any enjoyment out of the things I did	0	1	2	3
25	I was aware of the action of my heart in the absence of physical exertion (eg sense of heart rate increase, heart missing a beat)	0	1	2	3
26	I felt down-hearted and blue	0	1	2	3
27	I found that I was very irritable	0	1	2	3
28	I felt I was close to panic	0	1	2	3
29	I found it hard to calm down after something upset me	0	1	2	3
30	I feared that I would be 'thrown' by some trivial but unfamiliar task	0	1	2	3
31	I was unable to become enthusiastic about anything	0	1	2	3
32	I found it difficult to tolerate interruptions to what I was doing	0	1	2	3
33	I was in a state of nervous tension	0	1	2	3
34	I felt I was pretty worthless	0	1	2	3
35	I was intolerant of anything that kept me from getting on with what I was doing	0	1	2	3
36	I felt terrified	0	1	2	3
37	I could see nothing in the future to be hopeful about	0	1	2	3
38	I felt that life was meaningless	0	1	2	3
39	I found myself getting agitated	0	1	2	3
40	I was worried about situations in which I might panic and make a fool of myself	0	1	2	3
41	I experienced trembling (eg in the hands)	0	1	2	3
42	I found it difficult to work up the initiative to do things	0	1	2	3

The Calgary Depression Scale for Schizophrenia

(Addington *et al*, 1993)

Full information on the usage of this scale can be found at:
www.ucalgary.ca/cdss/
Reproduced with permission

Interviewer: Ask the first question as written. Use follow up probes or qualifiers at your discretion. Time frame refers to last two weeks unless stipulated.

NB: The last item, #9, is based on observations of the entire interview.

1. **DEPRESSION:** How would you describe your mood over the last two weeks? Do you keep reasonably cheerful or have you been very depressed or low spirited recently? In the last two weeks how often have you (own words) every day? All day?
   0. Absent
   1. Mild — Expresses some sadness or discouragement on questioning.
   2. Moderate — Distinct depressed mood persisting up to half the time over last two weeks: present daily.
   3. Severe — Markedly depressed mood persisting daily over half the time, interfering with normal motor and social functioning.

2. **HOPELESSNESS:** How do you see the future for yourself? Can you see any future? Or has life seemed quite hopeless? Have you given up or does there still seem some reason for trying?
   0. Absent
   1. Mild — Has at times felt hopeless over the last two weeks but still has some degree of hope for the future.
   2. Moderate — Persistent, moderate sense of hopelessness over last week. Can be persuaded to acknowledge possibility of things being better.
   3. Severe — Persisting and distressing sense of hopelessness.

3. **SELF-DEPRECIATION:** What is your opinion of your self compared with other people? Do you feel better, not as good, or about the same as others? Do you feel inferior or even worthless?
   0. Absent
   1. Mild — Some inferiority; not amounting to feeling of worthlessness.
   2. Moderate — Subject feels worthless, but less than 50% of the time.
   3. Severe — Subject feels worthless more than 50% of the time. May be challenged to acknowledge otherwise.

4. **GUILTY IDEAS OF REFERENCE:** Do you have the feeling that you are being blamed for something or even wrongly accused? What about? (Do not include justifiable blame or accusation. Exclude delusions of guilt.)
   0. Absent
   1. Mild — Subject feels blamed but not accused less than 50% of the time.
   2. Moderate — Persisting sense of being blamed, and/or occasional sense of being accused.
   3. Severe — Persistent sense of being accused. When challenged, acknowledges that it is not so.

5. **PATHOLOGICAL GUILT:** Do you tend to blame yourself for little things you may have done in the past? Do you think that you deserve to be so concerned about this?
   0. Absent
   1. Mild — Subject sometimes feels over guilty about some minor peccadillo, but less than 50% of time.
   2. Moderate — Subject usually (over 50% of time) feels guilty about past actions the significance of which s/he exaggerates.
   3. Severe — Subject usually feels s/he is to blame for everything that has gone wrong, even when not his/her fault.

6. **MORNING DEPRESSION:** When you have felt depressed over the last two weeks have you noticed the depression being worse at any particular time of day?
   0. Absent — No depression.
   1. Mild — Depression present but no diurnal variation.
   2. Moderate — Depression spontaneously mentioned to be worse in a.m.
   3. Severe — Depression markedly worse in a.m., with impaired functioning which improves in p.m.

7. **EARLY WAKENING:** Do you wake earlier in the morning than is normal for you? How many times a week does this happen?
   0. Absent — No early wakening.
   1. Mild — Occasionally wakes (up to twice weekly) 1 hour or more before normal time to wake or alarm time.
   2. Moderate — Often wakes early (up to 5 times weekly) 1 hour or more before normal time to wake or alarm.
   3. Severe — Daily wakes 1 hour or more before normal time.

8. **SUICIDE:** Have you felt that life wasn't worth living? Did you ever feel like ending it all? What did you think you might do? Did you actually try?
   0. Absent
   1. Mild — Frequent thoughts of being better off dead, or occasional thoughts of suicide.
   2. Moderate — Deliberately considered suicide with a plan, but made no attempt.
   3. Severe — Suicidal attempt apparently designed to end in death (ie: accidental discovery or inefficient means).

9. **OBSERVED DEPRESSION:** Based on interviewer's observations during the entire interview. The question, 'Do you feel like crying?' used at appropriate points in the interview, may elicit information useful to this observation.
   0. Absent
   1. Mild — Subject appears sad and mournful even during parts of the interview involving affectively neutral discussion.
   2. Moderate — Subject appears sad and mournful throughout the interview, with gloomy monotonous voice and is tearful or close to tears at times.
   3. Severe — Subject chokes on distressing topics, frequently sighs deeply and cries openly, or is persistently in a state of frozen misery if examiner is sure that this is present.

References

Addington D, Addington J & Maticka-Tyndale E (1993) 'Assessing depression in schizophrenia; the Calgary Depression Scale', *British Journal of Psychiatry*, 163 (22), pp39–44.

American Psychiatric Association (2000) *Diagnostic and Statistical Manual of Mental Disorders*, fourth edition, text revision: DSM-IV-TR, American Psychiatric Association, Washington DC.

Andreasen NC (1981) *The Scale for the Assessment of Negative Symptoms SANS*, University of Iowa, Iowa City, IA.

Andreasen NC (1982) 'Negative symptoms in schizophrenia definition & reliability', *Archives of General Psychiatry*, 39, pp784–8.

Andreasen NC (1984) *Scale for the Assessment of Positive Symptoms SAPS*, Department of Psychiatry, University of Iowa, Iowa City, IA.

Andresen R, Caputi P & Oades L (2006) 'Stages of recovery instrument: development of a measure of recovery from serious mental illness', *Australian and New Zealand Journal of Psychiatry*, 40, pp972–80.

Arntz A & Weertman A (1999) 'Treatment of childhood memories: theory and practice', *Behaviour Research & Therapy*, 37, pp715–40.

Asberg M, Montgomery SA, Perris C, Schalling D & Sedvall G (1978) 'A comprehensive psychopathological rating scale', *Acta Psychiatrica Scandinavica*, 57 (271) pp5–27.

Barkham M, Hardy GE & Startup M (1996) 'The 11P-32: A short version of the inventory of interpersonal problems', *British Journal of Clinical Psychology*, 35, pp21–35.

Bauer MS, Crits-Christoph P, Ball WA, Dewees E, McAllister T, Alahi P, Cacciola J & Whybrow PC (1991) 'Independent assessment of manic & depressive symptoms by self rating; scale characteristics and implications for the study of mania', *Archives of General Psychiatry*, 48 (9), pp807–12.

Bayley R (1996) 'First person account schizophrenia', *Schizophrenia Bulletin*, 22, pp727–9.

Bebbington P, Bhugra D & Brugha T (2004) 'Psychosis, victimisation and childhood disadvantage: evidence from the second British national survey of psychiatric morbidity', *British Journal of Psychiatry*, 185, pp220–6

Beck AT (1976) *Cognitive Therapy and Emotional Disorders*, International Universities Press, New York.

Beck AT, Epstein N, Brown G & Steer RA (1988) 'An inventory for measuring clinical anxiety: psychometric properties', *Journal of Consulting and Clinical Psychology*, 56 (6) pp893–7.

Beck AT, Steer RA & Brown GK (1996) *Manual for the Beck Depression Inventory-II*, Psychological Corporation, San Antonio, TX.

Beck AT, Rector NA, Stolar N & Grant P (2009) *Schizophrenia: Cognitive Theory, Research, and Therapy*, The Guildford Press, New York.

Berman I, Kalinowski A, Berman SM, Lengua J & Green AI (1995) 'Obsessive and compulsive symptoms in chronic schizophrenia', *Psychiatry*, 36, pp6–10.

Berman I, Merson A & Viegner B (1998) 'Obsessions and compulsions as a distinct cluster of symptoms in schizophrenia; a neuropsychological study', *Journal of Nervous Mental Disorders*, 186, pp150–6.

Bernstein EM & Putnam FW (1986) 'Development, reliability and validity of a dissociation scale', *Journal of Nervous and Mental Diseases*, 174, pp727–34.

Birchwood M (2003) 'Pathways to emotional dysfunction in first-episode psychosis', *British Journal of Psychiatry*, 182, pp373–5.

Birchwood M, Traver P, Brunet K, Gilbert P, Iqbal Z & Jackson C (2007) 'Social anxiety and the shame of psychosis: a study in first-episode psychosis', *Behaviour Research and Therapy*, 45, pp1025–37.

Blake DD, Weathers FW, Nagy LM, Kaloupek DG, Gusman FD, Charney DS & Keane TM (1995) 'The development of a clinician-administered PTSD scale', *Journal of Traumatic Stress*, 8 (1), pp75–90.

Blanchard JJ, Horan WP & Brown SA (2001) 'Diagnostic differences in social anhedonia: a longitudinal study of schizophrenia and major depressive disorder', *Journal of Abnormal Psychology*, 11, pp363–71.

Blanchard JJ, Kring AM, Horan WP & Gur R (2011) 'Towards the next generation of negative symptom assessments: the collaboration to advance negative symptom assessment in schizophrenia', *Schizophrenia Bulletin*, 37 (2), pp291–9

Blanchard JJ, Mueser KT & Bellack AS (1998) 'Anhedonia, positive and negative affect and social functioning in schizophrenia', *Schizophrenia Bulletin*, 24, pp413–24.+

Blazer DG, Kessler RC, McGonagle KA & Swartz MS (1994) 'The prevalence and distribution of major depression in a national community sample: the national comorbidity survey', *American Journal of Psychiatry*, 151, pp979–86.

Bleuler E (1911) 'Dementia Praecox or the Group of Schizophrenias', Aschaffenburg G (ed), *Handbuch der Psychiatrie*, Spezieller Teil 4, Leipzig, Deuticke.

BPS, *see* British Psychological Society.

Brewin CR, Andrews B & Valentine JD (2000) 'Meta-analysis of risk factors for posttraumatic stress disorder in trauma-exposed adults', *Journal of Consulting and Clinical Psychology*, 68, pp748–66.

Brewin CR, Dalgleish T & Joseph S (1996) 'A dual representation theory of posttraumatic stress disorder', *Psychological Review*, 23, pp339–76.

Brewin CR, Gregory JD, Lipton M & Burgess N (2010) 'Intrusive images in psychological disorders: characteristics, neural mechanisms and treatment implications', *Psychological Review*, 117 (1), pp210–32.

Brewin CR, Lanius RA, Novac A, Schnyder U & Galea S (2009) 'Reformulating PTSD for DSM-V. Life after criterion A', *Journal of Traumatic Stress*, 22 (5) pp366–73.

British Psychological Society (2000) *Understanding Mental Illness; recent advances in understanding mental illness and psychotic experiences*, Division of Clinical Psychology, The British Psychological Society.

British Psychological Society (2010) *Understanding Bipolar Disorder, Why Some People Experience Extreme Mood States and What Can Help*, Division of Clinical Psychology, The British Psychological Society.

Burns DD (1989) *The Feel Good Handbook, Using the New Mood Therapy in Everyday Life*, Morrow, New York, NY.

Cannon-Spoor HE, Potkin SG & Wyatt RJ (1982) 'Measurement of premorbid adjustment in chronic schizophrenia', *Schizophrenia Bulletin*, 8, pp470–84.

Carpenter WT, Heinrichs DW & Wagman AMI (1988) 'Deficit and non-deficit forms of schizophrenia: the concept', *American Journal of Psychiatry*, 145, pp578–83.

Cartwright-Hatton S & Wells A (1997) 'Beliefs about worry and intrusions: the Meta-Cognitions Questionnaire and its correlates', *Journal of Anxiety Disorders*, 11 (3), pp279–96.

Chadwick P, Birchwood M & Trower P (1996) *Cognitive Therapy for Delusions, Voices and Paranoia*, Wiley, Chichester, England.

Chapman LJ & Chapman JP (1978) 'Revised Physical Anhedonia Scale', unpublished test, University of Wisconsin, Madison, WI.

Chapman LJ, Chapman JP & Miller EN (1982) 'Reliabilities and intercorrelations of eight measures of proneness to psychosis', *Journal of Consulting and Clinical Psychology*, 50, pp187–95.

Chen W-C, Chu H, Lu R-B, Chou Y-H, Chen C-H, Chang Y-C, O'Brien PA & Chou K-R (2009) 'Efficacy of progressive muscle relaxation training in reducing anxiety in patients with acute schizophrenia', *Journal of Clinical Nursing*, 18 (15), pp2187–96.

Chisholm B, Keen N & Steel C (2010) 'Working with trauma and psychosis within a CBT framework' workshop, Reading, February 2010.

Clark DM & Wells A (1995) 'A cognitive model of social phobia', Heimberg R, Leibowitz M, Hope DA and Schneider FR (eds), *Social Phobia; Diagnosis Assessment and Treatment*, Guildford Press, New York, NY.

Cohen S, Kamarck T & Mermelstein R (1983) 'A global measure of perceived stress', *Journal of Health and Social Behaviour*, 24, pp385–96.

Cooper CL (1981) *The Stress Check*, Prentice Hall Spectrum, New Jersey.

Craig A, Hancock K & Craig M (1996) 'The lifestyle appraisal questionnaire: a comprehensive assessment of health and stress', *Psychology & Health*, 11 (3), pp331–43.

Cunningham BG, Owens DG, Miller P, Lawrie SM & Johnstone EC (2005) 'Pathogenesis of schizophrenia: a psychopathological perspective', *British Journal of Psychiatry*, 186, pp386–93.

Docherty NM, Cohen AS, Nienow TM, Dinzeo TJ & Dangelmaier RE (2003) 'Stability of formal thought disorder and referential communication disturbances in schizophrenia', *Journal of Abnormal Psychology*, 112 (3), pp469–75.

Dodd A, Mansell W, Tai SJ & Morrison AP (2011a) 'Factor structure of the hypomanic attitudes and positive predictions inventory in a student sample', *Personality and Individual Differences*, 50, pp349–54.

Dodd A, Mansell W, Morrison AP & Tai S (2011b) 'Extreme appraisals of internal states and bipolar systems: the hypomanic attitudes and positive predictions inventory', *Psychological Assessment*, 18.

Dyck DG, Short RA, Hendryx MS, Norell D, Myers M, Patterson T, McDonell MG, Voss WD & McFarlane WR (2000) 'Management of negative symptoms among patients with schizophrenia attending multiple-family groups', *Psychiatric Services*, 51 (4), pp513–9.

Eckblad M & Chapman L (1983) 'Magical ideation as an indicator of schizotypy', *Journal of Consulting and Clinical Psychology*, 51, pp215–25.

Eckblad ML, Chapman LJ, Chapman JP & Mishlove M (1982) *The Revised Social Anhedonia Scale*, unpublished test, University of Wisconsin, Madison, WI.

Ehlers A & Clark DM (2000) 'A cognitive model of posttraumatic stress disorder', *Behaviour Research and Therapy*, 38, pp319–45.

Ellison Z, van Os J & Murray R (1998) 'Special feature: childhood personality characteristics of schizophrenia: manifestations of, or risk factors for, the disorder?' *Journal of Personality Disorder*, 12 (3), 247–61.

Fenton WS & McGlashan TH (1986) 'The predictive significance of obsessive-compulsive symptoms in schizophrenia', *American Journal of Psychiatry*, 143, pp437–41.

Fenton WS & McGlashan TH (1991) 'Natural history of schizophrenia subtypes, II. Positive and negative symptoms and long-term course', *Archives of General Psychiatry*, 48 (11), pp978–86.

Fenton WS & McGlashan TH (1992) 'Testing systems for assessment of negative symptoms in schizophrenia', *Archives of General Psychiatry*, 49 (3) pp179–84.

Foa EB (1995) *The Posttraumatic Diagnostic Scale (PDS) Manual*, MN National Computer Systems, Minneapolis, MN.

Foa EB & Kozak MJ (1995) 'DSM-IV field trial: obsessive compulsive disorder', *American Journal of Psychiatry*, 143, pp437–41.

Foa EB, Kozak MJ, Salkovskis PM, Coles ME & Amir N (1998) 'The validation of a new obsessive compulsive disorder scale: the obsessive compulsive inventory (OCI)', *Psychological Asssessment*, 10, pp206–14.

Fowler DR, Garety PA & Kuipers E (1995) *Cognitive Behaviour Therapy for Psychosis: theory and practice*, Wiley, Chichester, England.

Foy DW, Sipprelle RC, Rueger DR & Carroll EM (1984) 'Aetiology of posttraumatic stress disorder in Vietnam veterans: analysis of pre-military, military and combat exposure influences', *Journal of Consulting and Clinical Psychology*, 52, pp79–87.

Ganesan V, Kumar R & Khanna S (2001) 'Obsessive-compulsive disorder and psychosis', *Canadian Journal of Psychiatry*, 46, pp750–3.

Gearon JS, Bellack AS & Tenhula WN (2004) 'Preliminary reliability and validity of the clinician administered PTSD scale for schizophrenia', *Journal of Consulting and Clinical Psychology*, 72 (1), pp121–5.

Goodwin F & Jamison KR (1990) *Manic-Depressive Illness*, Oxford University Press, New York, NY.

Grant PM & Beck AT (2009) 'Defeatist beliefs as a mediator of cognitive impairment, negative symptoms and functioning in schizophrenia', *Schizophrenia Bulletin*, 35 (4), pp798–806.

Gray JA (1994) 'A general model of the limbic system and basal ganglia: applications to schizophrenia and compulsive behaviour of the obsessive type', *Neurological Review*, 50, pp605–13.

Grey N, Young K & Holmes E (2002) 'Cognitive restructuring within reliving: a treatment for peritraumatic emotional "hotspots" in PTSD', *Behavioural and Cognitive Psychotherapy*, 30, pp37–56.

Hadfield S & Hasson G (2010) *How to be Assertive in Any Situation*, Prentice Hall Life, New Jersey.

Halperin S, Nathan P, Drummond P & Castle D (2000) 'A cognitive-behavioural group-based intervention for social anxiety in schizophrenia', *Australian and New Zealand Journal of Psychiatry*, 34, pp809–13.

Hamner MB, Frueh CB, Ulmer H, Huber MG, Twomey TJ, Tyson C & Arana GW (2000), 'Psychotic features in chronic posttraumatic stress disorder and schizophrenia: comparative severity', *Journal of Nervous and Mental Disease*, 188 (4), pp217–21.

Hardy A, Fowler D, Freeman D, Smith B, Steel C, Evans J, Garety P, Kuipers E, Bebbington P & Dunn G (2005) 'Trauma and hallucinatory experiences in psychosis', *Journal of Nervous and Mental Disorders*,193 (8), pp501–7.

Harvey PD, Koren D, Reichenberg A & Bowie CR (2006) 'Negative symptoms and cognitive deficits: what is the nature of their relationship?', *Schizophrenia Bulletin*, 32 (2), pp250–8.

Hirschfeld RMA, Williams JBW, Spitzer RL, Calabrese JR & Flynn BS (2000) 'Development and validation of a screening instrument for bipolar spectrum disorder: the mood disorder questionnaire', *American Journal of Psychiatry*, 157, pp1873–5.

Hodgson RJ & Rachman S (1977) 'Obsessional compulsive complaints', *Behaviour Research and Therapy*, 10, pp181–9.

Holmes TH & Rahe RH (1967) 'The social adjustment rating scale', *Journal of Psychosomatic Research*, 11, pp213–18.

Horowitz LM, Rosenberg SE, Baer BA, Vreno G & Villasenor VS (1988) 'Inventory of interpersonal problems: psychometric properties and clinical applications', *Journal of Consulting and Clinical Psychology*, 56, pp885–92.

Hwang MY & Opler LA (1994) 'Schizophrenia with obsessive-compulsive features: assessment and treatment', *Psychiatric Annals*, 24, pp468–72.

Jackson C, Trower P, Reid I, Smith J, Hall M, Townend M, Barton K, Jones J, Ross R, Russell R, Newton E, Dunn G & Birchwood M (2009) 'Improving psychological adjustment following a first episode of psychosis: A randomised controlled trial of cognitive therapy to reduce post psychotic trauma symptoms', *Behaviour Research and Therapy*, 47 (6) pp454–62.

Jaeger J, Bitter I, Czobor P & Volavka J (1990) 'The measurement of subjective experiences in schizophrenia: the subjective deficit syndrome scale', *Comprehensive Psychiatry*, 31 (3), pp216–26.

Janssen I, Krabbendam L & Bak M (2004) 'Childhood abuse as a risk factor for psychotic experiences', *Acta Psychiatrica Scandinavia*, 109, pp38–45.

Jones S (2004) 'Psychotherapy of bipolar disorder: a review', *Journal of Affective Disorders*, 80, pp101–14.

Jones S, Mansell W & Walker L (2006) 'Appraisal of hypomania-relevant experiences: development of a questionnaire to assess positive self-dispositional appraisals in bipolar and behavioural high risk samples', *Journal of Affective Disorders*, 93 (1), pp9–28.

Kabat-Zinn J (1990) *Full Catastrophe Living: How to Cope with Stress, Pain and Illness Using Mindfulness Meditation*, Dell Publishing, New York, NY.

Kanner AD, Coyne JC, Scharfer C & Lazarus R (1981) 'Comparison of two modes of stress measurement: daily hassles and uplifts vs major life events', *Journal of Behavioural Medicine*, 4, pp1–39.

Kay SR, Opler LA & Lindenmayer JP (1987) 'The positive and negative syndrome scale (PANSS): rationale and standardisation', *British Journal of Psychiatry*, 155 (7), pp59–65.

Kennerley H (1996) 'Cognitive therapy of dissociative symptoms associated with trauma', *British Journal of Clinical Psychology*, 35, pp325–40.

Kilcommons A & Morrison A (2005) 'Relationships between trauma and psychosis: an exploration of cognitive factors', *Acta Psychiatrica Scandinavica*, 112, pp351–9.

Kimhy D, Delespaul P, Ahn H, Cai S, Shikhman M, Lieberman JA, Malaspina D & Sloan RP (2010) 'Concurrent measurement of "real-world" stress and arousal in individuals with psychosis: assessing the feasibility and validity of a novel methodology', *Schizophrenia Bulletin*, 36 (6), pp1131–9.

Kingdon BL, Egan SJ & Rees CS (2012) 'The illusory beliefs inventory: a new measure of magical thinking and its relationship with obsessive compulsive disorder', *Behavioural and Cognitive Psychotherapy*, 40, pp39–53.

Kingdon DG & Turkington D (2004) *Cognitive Therapy of Schizophrenia*, Guildford Press, London.

Kirkpatrick B, Buchanan RW, McKenney PD, Alphs LD & Carpenter WT (1989) 'The schedule for the deficit syndrome: an instrument for research in schizophrenia', *Psychiatry Research*, 30, pp119–23.

Kirkpatrick B, Fenton W, Carpenter WT & Marder SR (2006) 'The NIMH-MATRICS consensus statement on negative symptoms' *Schizophrenia Bulletin*, 32, pp296–303.

Kobasa SC (1982) 'The hardy personality', Sanders G & Suls J (eds), *Social Psychology of Health and Illness*, Lawrence Erlbaum Associates, New Jersey.

Krabbendam L, Myin-G I, DeGraaf R, Vollebergh W, Nolen WA, Ledema J & Van Os J (2004) 'Dimensions of depression, mania and psychosis in the general population', *Psychological Medicine*, 34, pp1177–86.

Kruger S, Braunig P, Hoffler J, Shugar G, Borner I & Langkrar J (2000) 'Prevalence of obsessive-compulsive disorder in schizophrenia and significance of motor symptoms', *Journal of Neuropsychiatry and Clinical Neuroscience*, 12, pp16–24.

Kubany ES, Haynes SN, Abueg FR, Manke FP, Brennan JM & Stahura C (1996) 'Development and validation of the trauma-related guilt inventory (TRGI)', *Psychological Assessment*, 8, pp428–44.

Lake CR (2008) 'Disorders of thought are severe mood disorders: the selective attention deficit in mania challenges the Kraepelinian dichotomy – a review', *Schizophrenia Bulletin*, 34 (1), pp109–17.

Lam D, Jones S, Hayward P & Bright J (1999) *Cognitive Therapy for Bipolar Disorders: A Therapist's Guide to Concepts, Methods and Practice*, Wiley, Chichester.

Lazarus RS (1971) 'The concept of stress and disease', Leu L (ed), *Society, Stress and Disease*, 1, Oxford University Press, London.

Leary MR (1983) 'A brief version of the fear of negative evaluation scale', *Personality and Social Psychology Bulletin*, 9 (3), pp371–5.

Lee DA (2005) 'The perfect nurturer; a model to develop a compassionate mind within the context of cognitive therapy', Gilbert P (ed), *Compassion: Conceptualisation, Research and Use in Psychotherapy*, Routledge, UK.

Leff JP & Vaughn CE (1981) 'The role of maintenance therapy and relatives' expressed emotion in relapse of schizophrenia: a two-year follow-up', *British Journal of Psychiatry*, 139, pp102–4.

Lehman AF (1988) 'A study of the quality of life of the severely mentally ill', *International Journal of Social Psychiatry*, 44 (2) pp79–91.

Lockett H, Hatton J, Turner R, Stubbins C, Hodgekins J & Fowler D (2012) 'Using a semi-structured interview to explore imagery experienced during social anxiety for clients with a diagnosis of psychosis: an exploratory study conducted within an early intervention for psychosis service', *Behavioural and Cognitive Psychotherapy*, 40, pp55–68.

Lovibond SH & Lovibond PF (1995) *Manual for the Depression Anxiety Stress Scales, 2nd edn*, Psychology Foundation, Sydney.

Lysaker PH & Bell MD (1995) 'Negative symptoms and vocational impairment in schizophrenia: repeated measures of work performance over six months', *Acta Psychiatrica Scandinavica*, 90, pp205–8.

Malla AK & Norman RM (1992) 'Relationship of major life events and daily stressors to symptomatology in schizophrenia', *Journal of Nervous and Mental Disease*, 180, pp664–7.

Mansell W (2006) 'The hypomanic attitudes and positive predictions inventory (HAPPI): A pilot study to select cognitions that are elevated in individuals with bipolar disorder compared to non-clinical controls', *Behavioural and Cognitive Psychotherapy*, 34, pp467–76.

Mattick RP & Clark JC (1998) 'Development and validation of measures of social phobia, scrutiny fear and social interaction anxiety', *Behaviour Research and Therapy*, 36 (4), pp455–70.

McGorry PD, Chanen A, McCarthy E, Riel RV, McKenzie D & Singh BS (1991) 'Post traumatic stress disorder following recent-onset psychosis an unrecognised post psychotic syndrome', *Journal of Nervous and Mental Disease*, 179 (5), pp253–8.

Meichenbaum D (1975) 'Self-instructional methods', Kanfer FH & Goldstein AP (eds), *Helping People Change: A Textbook of Methods*, Pergamon, New York, NY.

Michail M & Birchwood M (2009) 'Social anxiety disorder in first episode psychosis; incidence, phenomenology and relationship with paranoia', *British Journal of Psychiatry*, 195, pp234–41.

Mishlove M & Chapman LJ (1985) 'Social anhedonia in the prediction of psychosis proneness', *Journal of Abnormal Psychology*, 94, pp384–96.

Monk TK, Flaherty JF, Ellen F, Hoskin K & Kupfer DJ (1990) 'The social rhythm metric: an instrument to quantify the daily rhythms of life', *Journal of Nervous and Mental Disease*, 178 (2), pp120–6.

Moritz S, Fricke S, Jacobsen D, Kloss M, Wein C, Rufer M, Katenkamp B, Farhumand R & Hand I (2004) 'Positive schizotypal symptoms predict treatment outcome in obsessive-compulsive disorder', *Behaviour Research and Therapy*, 42, pp217–27.

Morrison AP, Frame L & Larkin W (2003) 'Relationships between trauma and psychosis: a review and integration', *British Journal of Clinical Psychology*, 42, pp331–53.

Mueser K, Trumbetta S & Rosenberg S (1998) 'Trauma and PTSD in severe mental illness', *Journal of Consulting and Clinical Psychology*, 66, pp493–9.

Mueser KT, Rosenberg SD, Goodman LA & Trumbetta SL (2002)'Trauma, PTSD and the course of severe mental illness: an interactive model', *Schizophrenia Research*, 53 (1–2), pp123–43.

Mueser KT, Rosenberg SD, Xie H, Jankowski MK, Bolton EE, Lu W, Hamblen JL, Rosenberg HJ, McHugo GJ & Wolfe R (2008) 'A randomized controlled trial of cognitive-behavioral treatment for posttraumatic stress disorder in severe mental illness', *Journal of Consulting and Clinical Psychology*, 72 (2) pp259–71.

National Institute for Health and Clinical Excellence (2010) 'Schizophrenia: core interventions in the treatment and management of schizophrenia in adults in primary and secondary care', *The British Psychological Society & The Royal College of Psychiatrists.*

Neria Y, Bromet EJ, Sievers S, Lavelle J & Fochtmann LJ (2002) 'Trauma exposure and post-traumatic stress disorder in psychosis: findings from a first-admission cohort', *Journal of Consulting and Clinical Psychology*, 70 (1), pp246–51.

NICE, *see* National Institute for Health and Clinical Excellence.

Norman RMG & Malla AK (1993) 'Stressful life events and schizophrenia: 1: a review of the research', *British Journal of Psychiatry*, 162, pp161–6.

Nuechterlein KH & Dawson ME (1984) 'A heuristic vulnerability/stress model of schizophrenic episodes', *Schizophrenia Bulletin'*, 10 (2), pp300–312.

Packer S, Husted J, Cohen S & Tomlinson G (1997) 'Psychopathology and quality of life in schizophrenia', *Journal of Psychiatry and Neuroscience*, 22, (4), pp231–4.

Padesky CA (1994) 'Schema change processes in cognitive therapy', *Clinical Psychology and Psychotherapy*, 1 (5), pp267– 8.

Pallanti S, Quercioli L & Hollander E (2004) 'Social anxiety in outpatients with schizophrenia: a relevant cause of disability', *American Journal of Psychiatry*,161, pp53–8.

Perlick DA, Rosenheck RA, Kaczynski R, Swartz MS, Canive JM & Lieberman JA (2006) 'Components and correlates of family burden in schizophrenia', *Psychiatrica Servica*, 57, pp1117–25.

Phillips LJ, Edwards J, McMurray N & Francey S (2012) 'Comparison of experiences of stress and coping between young people at risk of psychosis and a non-clinical cohort', *Behavioural and Cognitive Psychotherapy*, 40, pp69–88.

Pini S, Cassano GB, Dell'Osso L & Amador XF (2001) 'Insight into illness in schizophrenia, schizoaffective disorder and mood disorders with psychotic features', *American Journal of Psychiatry*, 158, pp122–5.

Powell T (2010) *The Mental Health Handbook*, Speechmark Publishing, Brackley.

Powell TJ & Enright SJ (1990) *Anxiety and Stress Management*, Routledge, London and New York.

Rachman S (2003) *The Treatment of Obsessions*, Oxford University Press, Oxford.

Read J, Agar K, Argyle N & Aderhold V (2003) 'Sexual and physical assault during childhood and adulthood as predictors of hallucinations, delusions and thought disorder', *Psychology and Psychotherapy: Theory Research and Practice*, 76, pp1–22.

Read J, Van Os J, Morrison AP & Ross CA (2005), 'Childhood trauma, psychosis and schizophrenia: a literature review with theoretical and clinical implications', *Acta Psychiatrica Scandinavica*, 112, pp330–50.

Rector NA, Beck AT & Stolar N (2005) 'The negative symptoms of schizophrenia: a cognitive perspective', *Canadian Journal of Psychiatry*, 50 (5), pp247–57.

Rector NA, Seeman MV & Segal ZV (2003) 'Cognitive therapy for schizophrenia: a preliminary randomised controlled trial', *Schizophrenia Research*, 63 (1), pp1–11.

Reine G, Bernard D & Lancon C (1998) 'Depression scales in schizophrenia: a critical review', *Encephale*, 24 (6), pp530–40.

Romme MAJ & Escher ADMAC (1989) 'Hearing voices', *Schizophrenia Bulletin*, 15, pp209–16.

Rosenburg CM (1967) 'Complications of obsessional neurosis', *British Journal of Psychiatry*, 113, pp823–32.

Rothschild B (2000) *The Body Remembers: The Psychophysiology of Trauma and Trauma Treatment*, WW Norton, New York, NY.

Salkovskis PM, Wroe AL, Gledhill A, Morrison N, Forrester E, Richards C, Reynolds M & Thorpe S (2000) 'Responsibility attitudes and interpretations are characteristic of obsessive compulsive disorder', *Behaviour Research and Therapy*, 38, pp347–72.

Sanavio E (1998) 'Obsessions and Compulsions: the Padua inventory', *Behaviour Research and Therapy*, 26, pp169–77.

Sands JR & Harrow M (1999) 'Depression during the longitudinal course of schizophrenia', *Schizophrenia Bulletin*, 25 (1), pp157–71.

Schneider K (1925) 'Compulsive states in Schizophrenia', *Archive fur Psychiatrie und Nervenkrankeiten*, 74, pp93–107.

Selten JP, Sijben NE, Vanden-Bosch RJ, Omloo-Visser J & Warmerdam H (1993) 'The subjective experience of negative symptoms: a self-rating scale', *Comprehensive Psychiatry*, 34 (3), pp192–7.

Sensky T, Turkington D, Kingdon D, Scott JS, Scott J, Siddle R, O'Carroll M & Barnes TRE (2000) 'A randomised controlled trial of cognitive-behavioural therapy for persistent symptoms in schizophrenia resistant to medication', *Archives of General Psychiatry*, 57 (2), pp165–72.

Shafran R, Thordarson DS & Rachman S (1996) 'Thought-action fusion in obsessive compulsive disorder', *Journal of Anxiety Disorders*, 10, pp379–91.

Shaner A & Eth S (1989) 'Can schizophrenia cause posttraumatic stress disorder?', *American Journal of Psychotherapy*, 4, pp588–97.

Shepherd G, Boardman J & Slade M (2008) *Making Recovery a Reality*, Sainsbury Centre for Mental Health, London.

Smucker MR (2005) *Imagery Rescripting and Reprocessing Therapy (IPPT): A Treatment Manual for Adult Survivors of Childhood Sexual Abuse Experiencing PTSD*, International Trauma Institute, Milwaukee, WI.

Soraya S, Murray S, Oosthuizen PP, Emsley RA & Stein D (2003) 'Linking posttraumatic stress disorder and psychosis: a look at epidemiology, phenomenology and treatment', *Journal of Nervous and Mental Disease*, 191 (10), pp675–81.

Speilberger CD (1988) *State-Trait Anger Expression Inventory*, Psychological Assessment Resources, Odessa, FL.

Stein M, Fuetsch M, Muller N, Hofler M, Lieb R & Wittchen H (2001) 'Social anxiety and the risk of depression', *Archives of General Psychiatry*, 58, pp251–6.

Taiminen T, Huttunen J, Heila H, Henriksson M, Isometsa E, Kahkonen J, Tuominen K, Lonnqvist J, Addington D & Helenius H (2001) 'The schizophrenia suicide risk scale (SSRS): development and initial validation', *Schizophrenia Research*, 47, pp199–213.

Taylor S (1996) 'Meta-analysis of cognitive-behavioural treatments for social phobia', *Journal of Behaviour Therapy and Experimental Psychiatry*, 27, pp1–9.

Taylor S (2006) *Clinicians Guide to PTSD: A Cognitive-Behavioural Approach*, Guildford Press, New York, NY.

Verdoux H, Van Os J, Maurice-Tison S, Gay B, Salamon R & Bourgeois ML (1999) 'Increased occurrence of depression in psychosis-prone subjects: a follow-up study in primary care settings', *Comprehensive Psychiatry*, 40 (6), pp462–8.

Walker EF & DiForio D (1997) 'Schizophrenia: A neural diathesis-stress model', *Psychological Review*, 104, pp667–85.

Watanabe AG, Fukuda S, Hara H, Maeda Y, Ohira H & Shirakawa T (2006) 'Differences in relaxation by means of guided imagery in a healthy community sample', *Alternative Therapy Health Medicine*, 12 (2), pp60–6.

Watson D & Friend R (1969) 'Measurement of social-evaluative anxiety', *Journal of Consulting and Clinical Psychology*, 33, pp448–57.

Weathers FW, Huska JA & Keane TM (1991) *PCL-C for DSM-IV*, National Center for PTSD-Behavioural Science Division, Boston, MA. (Government document in the public domain).

Weisman AG, Nuechterlein KH, Goldstein MJ & Synder KS (2000) 'Controllability perceptions and reactions to symptoms of schizophrenia: a within-family comparison of relatives with high and low expressed emotion', *Journal of Abnormal Psychology*, 109, pp167–71.

Wells A (1997) *Cognitive Therapy of Anxiety Disorders. A Practice Manual and Conceptual Guide*, Wiley, Chichester.

Williams EE (2004) *Interventions for Schizophrenia*, Speechmark, Bicester.

Wing JK & Brown GW (1970) *Institutionalism and Schizophrenia: A Comparative Study of Three Mental Hospitals*, Cambridge University Press, London.

World Health Organization (1992) *Classification of Mental and Behavioural Disorders; Clinical Descriptions and Diagnostic Guidelines* (ICD-10), World Health Organization.

Young JE, Klosko JS & Weishaar M (2003) *Schema Therapy: A Practitioners Guide*, Guildford, New York, NY.

Zubin J & Spring B (1977) 'Vulnerability: a new view of schizophrenia', *Journal of Abnormal Psychology*, 86, pp260–6.

Index

Entries in **bold** refer to figures, tables or boxes.

For Product Safety Concerns and Information please contact our
EU representative GPSR@taylorandfrancis.com Taylor & Francis
Verlag GmbH, Kaufingerstraße 24, 80331 München, Germany